Secrets & Big News

Enabling people to be themselves at work

[ACKNOWLEDGEMENTS]

My love and personal thanks to a small group of folk who have said at one time, or another, 'you can do it' and/or excite me and/or bombard me with more ideas than there is time to deliver.

    Roy, Barbara, Sally and Stephen Nash

    Kay Allen, Phil Friend, Jean Irvine, Angela Kefford-Watson, Julia Middleton, Moira Mitchell, Jim Pollard, Karen Prince-Wright, Susan Scott-Parker, Ann Stead, Sally Ward.

    And most especially, Mark Jones.

Published by Kate Nash Associates
© Kate Nash 2014

ISBN: 978-0-9928984-0-3

Designed by Soapbox, www.soapbox.co.uk

Secrets & Big News

Enabling people to be themselves at work

Kate Nash OBE

[THE SPONSORS]

PwC's goal is to create a working environment in which everyone is comfortable being themselves and where people appreciate their own and other's strengths. Creating value through diversity is what makes us strong as a business. This report with its practical guidance around language and where to focus attention for greatest impact is therefore helpful to our efforts which we know must be purposeful, measured and sustained.

The Metropolitan Police serves and is made up from all communities in London. We are committed to inclusion and seek to build others confidence in us. We hope Secrets & Big News will help disabled colleagues to be themselves and encourage them to seek the support they need for them to give their best to London. We believe this work will positively assist disabled colleagues and those around them, to see the benefits and address perceived barriers, arising from sharing personal, sometimes sensitive information about their difference and needs.

Microlink empowers disabled people to fulfill potential by delivering end-to-end workplace adjustment processes to employers. Our employer clients know that a robust, 'no-fuss' workplace adjustment process is one of the best ways of supporting employees. Our work has direct impact on improved employee engagement which is why we are delighted to support this publication and its practical approach to drive fresh conversations.

We in Post Office are absolutely committed to having a workforce that reflects the communities in which we live and serve and we are proud to support our disabled employees with innovative solutions to workplace adjustments to accommodate their needs. We want people to thrive and be themselves at work and we want to make that as easy as possible for our employees with a health condition or disability. That is why we are delighted to support this new conversation about disability at work and look forward to trying out some of the big ideas.

When we were invited to get involved with this project we were really keen to give it our support. The time is absolutely right to enhance our conversation about disability between employers and employees. Using the research to support the language we use to talk about disability and health conditions will be fundamental for an inclusive organisation like BT. Our "Count Me In" campaign and our Disability Passports, as well as the many other tools and support mechanisms we have, are helping our people and our managers start this fresh conversation.

Kate Nash Associates

Kate Nash Associates is the UK's lead consultancy in the establishment and delivery of workplace disability networks and resource groups. In the last eight years we have set up, or supported the delivery of 300 workplace networks in the public and private sector across the UK.

The reach of these networks extends to several thousands of disabled employees. Their establishment is having a powerful effect on the vision and ambition of disabled talent.

Kate Nash Associates is also the fastest growing provider of personal development training for disabled employees as well as network leaders in the business and public sector. We are driving a new purposeful conversation between disabled employees for business benefit.

Building disability confidence: phase three

Employers are entering a third phase of building a sustainable culture for recruiting and developing disabled employees in the UK and globally.

The first phase was about legislation. It was about understanding and embedding the disability-specific equalities legislation first secured in the UK in 1995 and now harmonised under the Equality Act 2010.

The second phase was about employers: the process by which they have become, and continue to become, disability-confident organisations (often with the assistance of best practice tools and enabling products). That phase continues.

Meanwhile, the third phase has begun. It is about disabled employees creating a fresh conversation about how to get ahead at work, how to build personal resilience and how to be themselves at work for personal and business benefit.

Secrets & Big News is our latest contribution to support the third phase of change.

Contents

[INTRODUCTION]
Mind your language	9
Foreword: Building confidence from the inside out – Baroness Jane Campbell DBE	10
Secrets & Big News Advisory Board: Time to look at things differently	12
What's in Secrets & Big News?	14

[SECTION ONE]
A fresh conversation – Kate Nash OBE	15
• It's not where you start, its where you finish	15
• Why this project at this time?	15
• To share or not to share information	17
• Disability-confident disabled employees	19
• Is the word 'reasonable' reasonable?	21
• Why do we 'disclose' and 'declare'?	22

[SECTION TWO]
The research	24
• Views of Employees	24
• Key drivers in sharing information about disability	24
• Key resisters in sharing information about disability	24
• Why don't disabled people describe themselves as disabled?	25
• Are disabled employees clear why they are being asked?	25
• Knowledge of the legal definition of disability	25
• Reading the cultural 'mood music'	25
• Views of employers	27
• The key driver in monitoring	27
• Prevalence of monitoring and levels of accuracy	27
• Other data monitored	28
• The key challenges	28
• The purpose of data capture	28

[SECTION THREE]
15 big ideas for employers to try	30
• Your organisation is not different	30
• Help your people to manage a journey	31
• Know what you can measure	31
• Learn from 'standout' integrated campaigns	32
• Use external sources of data	32
• Bring different sources of data together	33
• Don't start with data, build a route-map	33
• Don't get bogged down in definition	34
• Get over "Chair envy"	35
• Don't 'disclose' or 'declare': share	36
• Understand the space between dignity and need	36
• Find your home-grown change-agents	37
• Encourage people to be themselves	37
• Remove 'reasonable' from the neon lights	38
• Think global, act local	38

[SECTION FOUR]
15 big ideas for disabled employees to try	39
• Don't prejudge monitoring	39
• Take your time	40
• Don't let definition be a barrier	40
• Don't be defined	40
• Talk to other disabled employees	41
• Enjoy the journey	42
• Be yourself – it gets easier	42
• Don't get hung up on disclosure	43
• Rehearse for 'chair-envy'	43
• Network	43
• Be disability confident	44
• Provide positive feedback	44
• Don't apologise	44
• Avoid being an inspiration	45
• Consider brand purple	46

[SECTION FIVE]
Case studies   **48**
- Shell – Be Yourself   48
- BT – The Passport / 'Count Me In' Campaign   50
- Civil Service – the value of sharing disability information   53
- Lloyds Banking Group – Systemic Grounds to Succeed   55
- Accenture – Disability: It Happens   57

[SECTION SIX]
A fresh response   **60**
- Fresher statistics   60
- The basics   60
- Key messages from the research   60
- Fresher monitoring   61
- Why do employers monitor?   62
- Anonymous sharing   63
- Formal recording systems   63
- Individual sharing with colleagues and line managers   63
- Building trust   64
- How to ask the questions   64
- Key messages from the research   66
- A fresher workplace adjustment process   67
- Tackling inconsistent processes   68
- What should the process be called?   68
- What is the average cost of workplace adjustments?   69
- What should a workplace adjustment process include?   70

[SECTION SEVEN]
Feeling disability confident now?   **71**
- From 'getting in', to 'getting on'   71
- Disability-confident employers   71
- Disability-confident employees   72
- Networks – what's in a name?   73
- The third phase of change – thanks for the warm-up   74

Postscript   **74**
Endnotes   **79**

[APPENDICES]
1. Secrets & Big News Advisory Board and project enablers   80
2. List of participating employers   81
3. Approach to the study   82
4. Executive summary of the top recommendations for employers   83
5. Disability confident employees – a matrix of understanding   85
6. The role of charities and advice giving agencies   87

The author   **90**

[INTRODUCTION]
Mind your language

This book is not about disability law, medicine or politics. We use the language that makes the most sense in our context.

Throughout this book we mostly use the terms 'disability' and 'health-condition'. Sometimes we refer to ill-health.

While most of our messages refer to how employees can access the workplace adjustment process, we have not attempted to distinguish between those employees who fall into the definition of disability within the Equality Act 2010 and those who do not (but may still benefit from the process by which employers can make it easier for them to be themselves and access adjustments to do their jobs productively). Neither do we distinguish between impairment and disability – these things are distinctly different and it is helpful to understand the difference. However it is not the role of this publication to do that. Therefore we have chosen to stick with the terms 'disability' and 'health-condition' as two of the words most used by employers and employees alike.

Some people, as our research will show, do not choose to use the language of disability and will never do so. This will often include deaf and hard of hearing employees. It may include employees who have an accident or experience a long-term illness. It may include employees who have had a recent medical diagnosis and may be sick for a while. It may include employees who have an inherited condition. It may include employees who experience a mental health condition for six months, three years or a lifetime. It may include people with life-threatening conditions, such as cancer. Or facial disfigurement… or dyslexia… or diabetes… or Aspergers…

This does not matter. This book is about what it means to be human, how employers can keep and retain talent and how employees can be who they are.

Meanwhile, for anyone wanting to read a memorable description about the difference between impairment and disability and the application of the social model of disability at work, we would recommend 'Why Are You Pretending to Be Normal?'[1]

[FOREWORD]

Building confidence from the inside out

Baroness Jane Campbell DBE

"The task is…not so much to see what no one has yet seen, but to think what nobody has yet thought, about that which everybody sees"—*Erwin Schrodinger*

When I graduated in 1983 with a first class Masters degree I landed my first job soon afterwards. Six months later I was told I was unemployable by my employer. I did not buy that and 30 years later, having enjoyed a fulfilling career I now enjoy shaping the laws of the land.

The challenges I faced then largely remain: communication breakdown. No employer felt able to ask me what I might need to maximise my effectiveness and, in turn, I was too self-conscious to ask for adjustments. The 'secrets' of a successful relationship alluded both of us. The possibilities of a shared solution were never realised. Thankfully my anger fuelled my determination and confidence to try again. I eventually secured a career that has taken me to the top but it could so easily been another story.

That haunting scenario came to mind as I read this study. As I turned the pages my spirits lifted. This report is an honest expose of the personal barriers that prevent both the disabled employee and employer from exploring opportunities without fear of reprisal. It lays bare the territory for greater understanding and, more importantly, it offers up solutions and ideas for change. This study is different. It dares disabled people and employers to share information, personal reservations, ideas and solutions.

This report is a definite requirement for the 21st-century employer who is looking to develop new and different talents within the workplace. The report draws upon the experiences of 55 employers who took part in the study. Between them they were able to reach out to 2,511 of their disabled employees to hear their stories, giving the report the gravitas to examine areas of deep concern for disabled staff who may, or may not, openly share information about their disability.

The report highlights the importance of gathering data on likely problematic areas – in recruitment, promotion, pay, reward and satisfaction levels. It acknowledges that anonymous surveys are often the best ways to encourage disabled people to share information and the return rate is markedly higher. However, is anonymity what we all want? Perhaps safe openness offers a more constructive solution? When both parties are informed the possibilities for successful change expand.

I like this study because it makes employers and employees think differently about human possibilities. It explores ideas for real inclusion at work. Like me, the study is provocative. It dares us to change the way we relate to one another, whilst taking care of our personal vulnerabilities. It is challenging and constructive.

Secrets & Big News builds a clear case for the UK and global organisations to better engage with their employees and shows how to ask for information in a more positive way. It demands that employers depart from questions about "how we can increase 'disclosure' and 'declaration' rates?" and move to those that start by asking what we really want to know: "how we can make it easier for people to be themselves at work and to ask for the adjustments they might need to be as effective as possible?" To do otherwise is to score an own goal. Ultimately people want to give of their best.

The government's Disability Confident campaign launched in 2013 has provided a fresh opportunity for employers to engage with their disabled talent and create new understanding about what the detail means. The concept, originally conceived by Business Disability Forum has been, and will remain, a helpful tool to drive cultural change.

We know that work is essential for all people's health and can contribute to their life chances. Work impacts on our wellbeing, our confidence and, most importantly, our purpose in life. Most people will experience disability at some point in their life.

As I reflect on my career, most of which has been devoted to the emancipation of disabled people, I've learnt a very simple truth – successful employers learn from their workforce. Disabled people are part of that workforce, learn from them how to realise a disability confident organisation.

Jane Campbell

[SECRETS & BIG NEWS ADVISORY BOARD]

Time to look at things differently

"When the facts change, I change my mind. What do you do, sir?"—John Maynard Keynes

The experience of disability and ill health is not one that many of us would, if given the choice, invite into our lives. And yet it happens all the time. In fact, the majority of disabled people (83%) will acquire their disability during their working lives.[2]

It can be enormously difficult to embrace a new identity, find new ways to make sense of an entirely different route through life than the one you expected or planned for and to learn how to manage your impairment at work. Moreover, most people will have to do these things at the same time as wanting to continue to be their best at work.

Government figures suggest that disabled people make up 12.9% of the public sector workforce and 11% of the private sector.[3] However, employers who examine their own data and conduct internal surveys tell us that their figures are far lower than the national average suggests.

Where are the missing people? Why don't more people tell their employer about their disability or health condition? What is stopping people from sharing information with their employer?

The monitoring merry-go-round

Employers want to collect data for many reasons. But failure to collect accurate and meaningful data about disabled employees may result in no action, or the wrong action.

Surveys that result in very few people identifying as having a disability may reinforce a cultural belief that very few disabled people, or people with a health condition work for the organisation. Low numbers may also lead to inaccurate assumptions that disabled people don't want to or can't work well in certain trades or sectors. It may then lead to disproportionate efforts to recruit disabled people externally – "we better 'fix this' by recruiting disabled people because we aren't employing any".

Starting with purpose

Having been appointed as Advisors to the SBN Project Board, our role has been to support Kate Nash Associates in creating practical ideas for employers and employees to try. Our desire is to help shape a more positive landscape for both disabled employees and their colleagues.

Although the Secrets & Big News project wasn't designed to be an Employers Guide, we did begin the process thinking that the employer part of the report would include simple practical advice on monitoring. We have landed in a different place entirely. This report is in fact about why employers should build meaningful disability engagement strategies that will benefit the business and the individual. It then offers some big ideas for employers and employees to try.

We have identified the key reasons why disabled people find it hard to share information about their disability with their employer, and the things that would make it easier for them to do so.

Through the project we:

- Created a repository where employers and employees could share confidential information so we could pull out the common themes and share the 'enduring truths' for both employers and disabled employees
- Invited a fresh conversation about the subject of data capture through which we looked beyond change driven by statistics (which may not be accurate) to focus on equipping, enabling and realising potential
- Offered reminders about language, confidentiality, personal identity and how people feel about sharing information at work
- Pulled out the things it takes to engender trust and confidence between employers and disabled employees so people are comfortable about sharing

information, knowing what the employer will, and won't, do with it
- Have generated 15 big ideas for employers and employees – offering practical tips for both the organisational and individual journey of becoming disability-confident.

Looking at things differently

The board, with our extensive experience in driving change for disabled employees in our own and other organisations, and in driving broad cultural change programmes within the workplace, are inviting employers to look at things differently.

In 2015 it will have been 20 years since the passing of anti-discrimination legislation for disabled people. The original 1995 act established the principle of workplace adjustments as an integral part of what civil society deems a fair and just way of enabling great talent to secure and retain work.

In our view it is timely to reflect on those things that make it easier for people to be themselves at work in order to be the best most productive individuals they can be and be accepted with their difference, without resentment.

It has become clear that not all sharing of information about disability and adjustment is the same and may involve separate processes and personal decisions to share or otherwise. Sharing disability information for monitoring purposes is frequently mixed up with sharing information on disability linked to adjustment need or simply informing your colleagues about your difference. It shouldn't be.

Importantly we must consider the impact we create, as individuals and as organisations, when we use language or systems that are clumsy or meaningless or, far worse, lead to valuable employees feeling nervous, fearful or worthless.

There has never been a better time to highlight the benefits of work – but that can only be done by highlighting the practical things that can support individuals at work. That includes dealing with the human resisters head-on.

Our sincere thanks to the 55 employer partners and 2,511 disabled employees who worked with us and who are keen to encourage people to be themselves at work. We dedicate their efforts to the millions more across the UK who deserve to be so.

Advisory Board

Brendan Roach
Business Disability Forum

Robert Tate
Business in the Community

Matthew Thomas
Coca Cola

Sally Ward
BT

Paul Willgoss
Civil Service Disability Network

Joanna Wootten
Solutions Included

Angela Kefford Watson
Kate Nash Associates

John Turner
Lloyds Banking Group

Andy Garrett
Metropolitan Police

Andy Kneen
Shell

What's in *Secrets & Big News*?

The report is divided into 7 sections:

[ONE]
A FRESH CONVERSATION
Kate Nash OBE, the report's author, outlines some of the key blocks and drivers for change 20 years after the Disability Discrimination Act came into force. It helps set the scene for the rest of the report and invites us to notice the human resisters that play out in the lives of employees.

[TWO]
THE RESEARCH
This is a summary of the research findings from both the employers and employees. It highlights the key findings and drives the messages contained in the rest of the report including the 15 big ideas for employers and employees to try and elsewhere in the publication.

[THREE]
15 BIG IDEAS FOR EMPLOYERS
This section offers 15 big ideas for employers. Using the results from the research, this section busts some of the myths that still surround the subject of monitoring but also touches on the broader experience of disabled employees at work. The 15 big ideas are for employers to discuss, debate, to try out for size, to build on or throw out.

[FOUR]
15 BIG IDEAS FOR EMPLOYEES
This section offers 15 big ideas for disabled employees. Using the results from the research, this section busts some of the myths that surround subject of intent of employers when it comes to monitoring. The 15 big ideas are for employees to discuss, debate, to try out for size, to build on or throw out.

[FIVE]
CASE STUDIES
This section offers some case studies from the employer partners. Each of them illustrates different ways of building meaningful employee engagement. The case studies describe the issue being addressed, idea, drivers, resources, overcoming resistance, deliverables and benefits.

[SIX]
A FRESH RESPONSE
This section looks at what we can count when it comes about disability in the workplace, offers an overview of the key things to get right when monitoring disability at work and looks at how to improve one of the most critical enablers to support people in work – the workplace adjustment process.

[SEVEN]
FEELING DISABILITY CONFIDENT NOW?
The report closes with a view about where we can move the debate from 'getting in' to 'getting on'. It suggests we look at specific models for what we mean by disability confidence for employers and employees alike and invites us to build more pace in the development of inclusive employment practices.

It suggests where the next drivers for positive change will come from and invites our participation in the third phase of change regarding the employment of disabled people.

[SECTION ONE]

A FRESH CONVERSATION

Kate Nash OBE

"The most serious mistakes are not being made as a result of wrong answers. The truly dangerous thing is asking the wrong question"—*Peter Drucker*

It's not where you start, it's where you finish

When we started talking about this project we thought it would be a simple three step process. Firstly we would research the reasons why people find it hard to share information about health and disability. Then we would examine the ways employers monitor their workforces and collect data. Then we would bring the two together and offer simple advice about how to ask better questions to get more accurate data. However, we went on a different journey and where we have finished is with an invitation.

The invitation is for us all to think a bit more deeply about the human resisters that exist when we want to change the landscape for our disabled employees. It is an invitation to take a fresh look at what we can do differently to encourage disabled people to be who they are and to be the best of themselves at work. But before we invite you on that journey let us start at the beginning.

Why this project at this time?

For the last eight years Kate Nash Associates has been creating conversations between disabled employees within and across organisations of every size, sector and type of trade.

We help employers to set up networks or business resource groups and we help them to do this with a clear aim in mind – to help talented disabled employees be themselves, give their best, nurture their career and to notice and support pipeline talent too. Many networks help their organisation become disability-confident too. We have worked with many thousands of disabled employees at every level and in every business across the UK and internationally.

More than a quarter of the 28 million workers in the UK manage a long-term health condition or impairment.[4] If we relied on current levels

> **This publication is about how people flourish at work and what makes it easier or harder for them to do so**

of disability information shared at work or looked at media portrayals to present the picture of disability at work, we would be forgiven for thinking that the number was far less.

Much of the current public narrative about disability gets caught up with the debate on cost – the cost of welfare reform and the work programme, the cost of bedroom tax, the reduction of the funding available to fund the extra cost of disability through the introduction of Personal Independent Payments and the size of the national bill on social care. If it's not a story about cost, it's very often a story about the sporting achievements of Paralympian athletes or of disability brought on in dramatic circumstances such as the case of injured service personnel.

These are very important stories that offer huge insights about human endeavour and resilience. And they require a sophisticated journalistic approach to tease out the bits of information that provide helpful learning. But most of the public narrative about disability offers little that is relevant to the majority of disabled employees in the UK.

We don't get to hear about the debate on talent and the lived experience of disabled employees who work day in, day out, in every organisation in the UK. How do they move themselves through medical diagnosis and a period of adjustment at the same time as doing the day job? How do they move their colleagues on? Why and how do the vast majority of them never even entertain the idea of job loss and a life on benefits? How do they feel about sharing information about their health or disability? How do they build individual resilience? What is their view as to how the experience of difference adds value to their skills and competencies? How do they feel about sometimes being role models and catalysts for change within their own organisation?

Through our work with nearly 300 organisations that have disability networks or business resource groups we know at first-hand how committed many employers are at wanting to recruit, retain and develop their disabled employees.

But we also know how many of them worry about how to get accurate and reliable information about the number of disabled people they employ. Some employers struggle to justify a fresh strategic approach to cultural and systems change because their 'declaration' or 'disclosure' rates are so low, or it appears to be expensive, or there are just so many other important issues so why bother with this one?

From day one of the introduction of the Disability Discrimination Act 1995 (now harmonised under the Equality Act 2010) we all knew the definition of disability would create challenges for both employers and individuals alike. But it was a pragmatic choice at the time whatever hindsight might suggest.

But, nearly two decades later, who among us could have predicted the level of confusion the word 'disability' would bring to employers and individuals alike? And with all that experience what can employers now do differently and better to reduce the anxiety that so many people have about sharing information either formally, or informally?

My driver in writing this is our need for a new approach to the subject often referred to as 'declaration' and 'disclosure' but which is really about why and how people will choose to share information about their disability at work.

To share or not to share information

We've said that disability and ill health are experiences that few would choose invite into their lives. It can be enormously difficult to embrace a new identity, or learn different ways of getting through life, or making sense of an entirely different trajectory to the journey you expected to take in life. And that is not to mention the myriad of ways that different disabled people have to manage their impairment in and outside of work.

But this publication is not about the individual psychology of those things. It is about how people flourish at work and what makes it easier or harder for them to do so. It is about how we can shift the paradigm away from what people cannot do, towards an enabling approach that focuses on how they can be their best at work.

Gilly's story

While writing this, I received an email from the CEO of a reputable not-for-profit organisation who I've known for about 25 years. She was asking for my advice about how her daughter might approach a problem she was facing at work. Her daughter, Gilly, has a physical impairment and is in her mid 20s.

Gilly had recently been promoted. While her boss knew about her health condition, she/he suggested, in view of her promotion, that the time was right to let HR know her situation as it hadn't come to light during the recruitment process. She took this advice, told the head of HR who then sent out an email to the management team, telling them about her health condition in great detail.

As you can imagine, Gilly was devastated and desperate not to be seen as weak or needy. She was then contacted by phone to do a risk assessment, which took half an hour. The risk assessor asked what drugs Gilly was taking and she told him. The immediate question from the risk assessor was "if you are on all these drugs, how could you say you are well?" He then said unless she gave him permission to tell the management that he would not pass her fit for work.

What should she do? How would you advise her? Your views may have changed after you've read this document. You can see what I wrote in the postscript on page 77.

A rock and a hard place

There are many thousands of people just like Gilly – people who, if given the choice, would probably prefer not to experience disablement but do, and at the same time they still want to succeed and flourish at work: especially when work is such an important aspect of a person's self worth and identity. The same people may live in fear that if their colleagues know about their disability they might assume that it will have a negative impact on their ability to work.

This experience is played out thousands of times every year, right now, in every workplace in the UK and globally. But very few of us will find

» **It can be enormously difficult to embrace a new identity, or learn different ways of getting through life**

quick ways of learning the skills to navigate our way through other people's fear, pity, lack of expectation or rejection. These things take time to learn. People have little opportunity to practice the art of 'being different' or to become a disability-confident individual. The absence of this opportunity is the 'missing link' in any sustainable system change designed to get disabled people in work and more especially to retain work. After all, we all work best when we are authentic, do not have to act and can bring our true personality to work.

Put simply, we hear a lot about disability-confident employers. But disability confidence works both ways. The employment rate of known disabled employees has remained stubbornly low. While disabled people are now more likely to be employed than they were in 2002, disabled people remain significantly less likely to be in employment than non-disabled people. In 2012, 46.3% of working age disabled people were in employment compared to 76.4% of working age non-disabled people.[5] The time is right to look beyond the rocks and the hard places.

The 'rock' is the need employers often have to pigeon hole, to label, to work out "who these people are" and having done so, to demonstrate it in numbers (the 'disclosure rates' of disability). The 'hard place' is length of time it often takes us, as disabled people, to make sense of and accommodate an impairment – and then share that information at the same time as preserving dignity and building resilience.

Secrets & Big News is all about these things. It is about what employers can do to make it easier for people to share information about disability. This is a key step towards people being able to be who they are, get the adjustments they might need and continue to give of their best.

But we don't stop there. This report is also about what individuals who experience ill-health, disability, accident or injury can do too.

Where's the good advice?

There is little good advice available to people in work on what to do about sharing information concerning disability, health conditions, an accident or injury with your employer.

There is no 'one-stop-shop' agency about whether to share such information with your employer, or indeed when and how to do so. Where do you go for advice when your employer seems to be suggesting that you have been hiding something you would prefer not to have?

When the project team searched what was available – from employers, employer service providers, disability campaigning organisations, business-led membership organisations, social media chat rooms, external consultants, well-known disabled thought-leaders – most of the 'advice' boils down to five messages:

- Disabled people are protected from discrimination by the Equality Act 2010;
- Disabled people are not obliged to tell their employer about their disability and there may be advantages and disadvantages to sharing personal information;
- You are obliged to tell your employer information about yourself that may be relevant to any safety critical aspect of your job;

- The outcomes of sharing information are sometimes positive, but not always;
- By sharing information with your employer you are protected by the Equality Act and can request a workplace adjustment.

One of the things that alarm me about these messages is that they feel nervous and undecided. They offer little about the benefits of sharing information as part of the process of getting what you might need to be effective at work. Could it be that some of the advice givers themselves are unsure of the value of disabled talent?

An example of this is when it's sometimes suggested that in making a decision about whether to share information about disability, folk should look for 'clues' or 'indicators' as to how 'inclusive' the employer is or how supportive their manager/team/business unit is likely to be before they share information. Why aren't we focusing more on the benefits of being disability-confident?

The clues that are often cited for individuals to 'test' the level of how 'inclusive' the employer is with regard to disability are: whether the employer is a member of Business-to Business membership organisations, whether the employer audits their recruitment processes for accessibility, whether the employer offers targeted recruitment programmes such as disabled graduate internships schemes, whether the employer uses the Two Tick disability symbol. And so the list goes on.

I understand why this advice is given. Nobody wants to advise anyone to do something that might make their situation worse but in doing this, a difficult situation is rendered more confusing. Times are changing. A little boldness is needed from us all – including advice-giving agencies.

The existing 'advice' is impractical. It is unrealistic to leave people to find out this information before deciding to share sensitive information and especially so for those learning to manage a new health or disability experience with limited levels of certainty. Moreover, the timidity seems to erode the basic principle that employers have a duty not to discriminate against disabled people.

Our research suggests one in five disabled people seek external advice about whether to share information. If an employee is looking outside the organisation for guidance on whether to share information about their disability with their employer, there is already something seriously wrong or missing. The current advice is not doing a lot to fill that gap.

To be blunt, how helpful would this ambivalent and nervous advice be to someone like Gilly?

Disability-confident disabled employees

The Equality Act 2010 harmonised legislation which means it is illegal to discriminate against anyone because of different protected characteristics (for example age, being pregnant or having a child, religion/belief or lack of religion/belief and so on[6]). And while there are different considerations to take in to account in terms of employability and the barriers that exist, it is unusual to see ambivalent 'advice' about sharing information about protected characteristics.

» **A little boldness is needed from us all**

For example, in a monitoring exercise based on gender balance, most employers will have strong participation rates. It would be hard to envisage a situation where women would look for external advice about whether to share such information before doing so. The era of women having to disguise themselves as men or take a male name to get employment has passed. And you certainly don't see nervous advice from the Fawcett Society with a long list of pros and cons about sharing whether you are a woman when you apply for a job.

Of course, these things are complex. With sexual orientation, or religion and belief there are similar concerns around discrimination when individuals choose to share information. But perhaps the era of disabled people having to effectively disguise themselves is coming to an end too.

In deciding whether to take the step to share information or not, employees weigh up the risks and benefits of sharing versus maintaining the status quo and not sharing. No two people will view this in the same way. There are a number of factors, such as the perceived impact of sharing, the actual observed impact of others sharing, the anticipated reactions from colleagues and the level of support available. All need to be carefully considered.

For me, it is the often lengthy process of assimilating and making sense of disability and impairment which results in renegotiating many different parts of your life and about doing things differently that causes the rub. Acquiring a health condition or disability can sometimes impact on colleagues. The experience sometimes requires an action that may cost or inconvenience someone else.

Moreover the experience often means a change in identity – sometimes subtle, sometimes profound, and nearly always uninvited.

A friend once told to me that he was the first disabled person he had ever met – describing vividly the isolation that often comes with the realisation that everything you once took for granted has disappeared.

The knowledge that to remain valued, efficient and productive at work you may have to request an action that will cost or inconvenience someone else while at the same as managing a shift in identity, comes only from practice, experience and conversation with others who have done the same. It comes from internal confidence. And it sometimes comes from the love and assurances from friends, family and colleagues that you are still worthy and valuable and deserve your space on earth.

Levels of learning individual confidence

The majority of disabled people, and those with a health condition, will acquire their disability (or be diagnosed for the first time) through the course of their employment. Disabled people make up 12.9% of the public sector workforce and 11% of the private sector.[7]

This means every workforce has a significant proportion of people who are making sense of something they didn't readily invite into their lives, something that may not be static and which they may be requiring them to navigate a range of variables and new experiences (eg. new communication needs, new mobility needs, new resilience needs, new expectations or lack of expectations of others). And, on top of it all, often a new uncertainty about what life will offer and what it means to be human in these new circumstances.

It is very hard to share information about something of which you are still making sense, of which you may not understand the long term effects and, crucially, which you would prefer not to have.

Using a very personal example, if you had asked me whether I was a disabled person in the first 10 years of my life with arthritis I would not have known how to answer you. Back then I was active in the political process of securing anti-discrimination legislation but I knew profoundly that while physical access issues would forever be a potential barrier to career success, it was the soft bigotry of low expectation from others about me that would be the trump card in whether I would get in and get on at work.

Even worse, it was dawning on me that I had an active role to play in whether I allowed other peoples' perceptions to get in the way.

After 35 years with a disability and of having been close to the process of securing anti-discrimination legislation in the UK, I believe we should now turn our head to fundamentally address some of the human resisters of the type that Gilly experienced. Many employers are already doing so and are creating imaginative cultural change programmes that don't rely on the 'one-size fits all' school of equalities training. However Gilly's experience is so commonplace that we possibly take it for granted that nothing can be done to support disabled employees to be themselves – often their new 'selves'.

Might it be possible, desirable even, to create the circumstances for employers to help disabled employees to make more sense of their disability in the context of work? In effect, to make it easier for them and their managers/colleagues to share their expectations about what it means to become disability confident at work? Nobody wants to walk on egg-shells at work.

Is the word 'reasonable' reasonable?

Employment law has established the concept of 'reasonable adjustments' as a duty for employers. It is rare to meet any employer who has not heard of the term and what it can mean.

True, a significant number of employers are struggling to skill up their people about the methods and practical things that can be done to help people retain their job often at low, or no, cost. But the concept is "out there" and well known.

One of the things that struck me during our research was how many employers were questioning whether there is a better way to convey intent when devising communication messages than putting the word "reasonable" everywhere. When you see 'reasonable' in neon lights everywhere you don't see 'adjustment' and it's the adjustment that matters. Could adjusting our approach to adjustments provide better outcomes? It seems employers are beginning to think so too.

We don't talk about "reasonable" maternity cover. We talk about maternity cover.

We don't talk about "reasonable" health and well-being policies. We talk about health and well-being policies.

> » **It is very hard to share information about something of which you are still making sense, of which you may not understand the long term effects and, crucially, which you would prefer not to have**

> **Why have disabled employees not challenged the potential over-use of the term 'reasonable adjustment' process?**

We don't talk about 'reasonable' flexible or remote working policies, we talk about flexible or remote working policies.

We take it for granted that an employer believes these 'adjustments' to be reasonable and they will work out the formula.

And yet, when it comes to disability, the majority of employers refer to the adjustment process as the 'reasonable adjustment process' in their policies, procedures and communications. It may be a helpful concept when the employer 'machine' considers its ability to make the adjustments for people, taking cost, disruption and health and safety into account but it does seem somewhat odd to use as a standard phrase.

We don't prefix other employment policies with a word that suggests we have pre-determined the conclusion so why do employers do it with workplace adjustments?

Could it be that we just lacked imagination when the legislation was first passed? Could it be that our human resource and diversity professionals in their desire to get moving on policies, forgot the need to brand them internally and communicate the purpose with a bit of flair? Or was it that this legislation was such a fundamental shift, we could not quite let go of the fact that the adjustments had to be at a reasonable cost and dared not suggest otherwise? Would that have been too great a leap to make?

Even more intriguing why have disabled employees not challenged the potential over-use of the term 'reasonable adjustment' process? Is there a level at which we, too, are not convinced of our worth that we concede the need for employers to prefix the process with a reminder that they will decide if the adjustments are affordable or practicable for the organisation?

Encouragingly, our study does show that a good smattering of employers are starting to refer routinely to "workplace adjustments" rather than "reasonable adjustments." I think this will make it easier for people to ask for the adjustments they may need and it will have impact over time.

What attracts me is the possibility of making a real impact on the number of people who feel able to ask for and source an adjustment process by calling it something else.

Why do we 'disclose' and 'declare'?

If you do an online search on the terms 'disclosure' and 'declaration' you can see plenty of pieces written by disabled thought-leaders or disability-confidence consultants. In fact many of the most well-known "game changers" working in the UK will have something to say on the topic. But none have so far questioned the very terms 'disclosure' and 'declaration' and most of them use them on their websites, at conferences, during training programmes.

What we wanted to do was give us all the opportunity to think about the impact of our use of this language on all of the stakeholders in an organisation, including risk assessors like the one who called Gilly. We have been asking ourselves lots of questions.

- Why do people really use the terms 'declaration' and 'disclosure' when referring to data capture?
- What would happen if we stopped using the words?

- What impact would it have if employers together with disability networks and resource groups encouraged disabled employee colleagues to share information about their disability?
- Would any of these things lead to more people being harassed? Victimised? Bullied? Dismissed? Or would it help employers to notice where they had more work to do to support line mangers to deliver the adjustments aimed at enabling great performance?
- Could switching the language and narrative with something more positive, create cultural shifts away from rights and towards enabling performance, akin to that with non-disabled talent?
- Could more positive processes help bust some myths, reduce fear of negative consequences and build disability confidence?

The employers we worked with throughout the course of this project are truly on a mission. They don't want to inadvertently give the impression to employees that they are 'disclosing' a secret or a big piece of news, even when those same employees think so themselves. Similarly the 2,511 disabled workers are on a mission to be themselves.

It is this that lies at the heart of our messages to come: how we can encourage valuable employees to be themselves at work. When employers do this they get to hear more quickly about the adjustments they can make, can deliver them faster and can be rewarded by keeping people productive, efficient and good at their jobs.

[SECTION TWO]

THE RESEARCH

"We inhabit a world in which we tend to put labels on each other and expect that we will then march through life wearing them like permanent sandwich boards"—Nick Webb

TO SHARE OR **NOT TO SHARE**
information about their disability with their employer

YES — Why? — NO

57% needed their employer to make an adjustment for them

60% worried that there may be repercussions either now, or in the future

WORRIED ABOUT REPERCUSSIONS
either now, or in the future

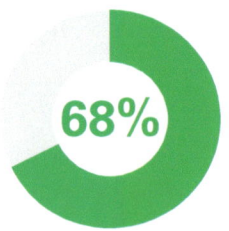

68%
Public sector employees

50%
Private sector employees

We conducted the study in two parts. One part was to determine the broad practice of monitoring across the public and private sector and to seek the views and experiences of employers including their challenges and concerns.

The second part was to seek the views and experiences of disabled employees and to hear first-hand what makes it easier or challenging to share information about disability and ill-health at work.

55 employers took part and 2,511 disabled employees were reached.

Views of Employees

Employer partners circulated the employee survey as widely as they could. We allowed them the freedom to do this in any way they could. Some sent out a global message across the organisation, some to those employees who had requested or secured an adjustment and some to those people who were involved in a disability network or business resource group. Some employers did all three. As a result 2,511 employees took part.

Key drivers in sharing information about disability

The majority of respondents (57%) said that the main reason they shared information about their disability was that they needed their employer to make an adjustment for them. This seems to suggest that there needs to be a practical reason why people choose to share personal information such as an adjustment need.

Conversely one of the reasons why employees may not share information is that they do not need a workplace adjustment and thereby saw no reason why they should share something that did not require an action.

Key resisters in sharing information about disability

Of those respondents who had not shared information about their disability with their employer the vast majority of respondents (60%) said that the main reason why they did not do so is that they would be worried that if they told their employer there may be repercussions either now, or in the future. Those in the public sector are more worried about repercussions (68%) than those in the private sector (50%).

Others do not feel the need to share information either because they do need any adjustment made in the way they did their job (22%) or it is not seen as relevant to tell their employer (15%).

In fact, 3 in 4 disabled employees when deciding to tell anyone about their disability, illness, injury or accident take into account how others may react either now, or in the future.

Survey respondents repeatedly expressed views that suggested that for them the decision to identify with disability or ill-health was an 'emotional' transaction. It required thought, reflection and anticipation about what might follow as a consequence.

Why don't disabled people describe themselves as disabled?

Employees are very cautious about their association with the word 'disability'. Nearly two-thirds (63%) believe that either some people will always resist the label or think the association with the word is a big personal step.

A Department for Work and Pensions report in 2013 (Fullfilling Potetnial) demonstrated the diverse experience of disability and the different meanings it has for everyone. Their research suggested that of the 11 million people with a health condition or impairment that are protected from discrimination by the disability provisions of the UK's equality law, only one quarter describe themselves as disabled. When we asked the respondents why they thought this was the case, 36% suggest it is a big personal step to associate yourself with the word disability. A further 27% say that some people will always resist the label of 'disability' because it feels so negative. Another 22% said it takes a long time to understand that what you are experiencing is the same as the Equality Act's definition of disability or indeed to understand the benefits of being covered by the definition.

Are disabled employees clear why they are being asked?

Opinion is polarised as to why their employer asks for information about disability, with 42% of those asked, not knowing why. And perhaps more significantly, nearly half of the survey respondents (47%) do not understand how their employer will use the information.

Knowledge of the legal definition of disability

Only 52%, just over half of the respondents, knew the definition of disability in the Equality Act (or the legal definition in the country where they worked) before sharing information. Public sector employees are significantly more likely to be aware – 59% as opposed to 41% in the private sector.

Reading the cultural 'mood music'

Three-quarters (75%) of respondents either strongly agree or agree that when deciding whether to tell anyone about their disability, illness, injury or accident they take into account their view of how others may react to them either now, or in the future. This includes their view of how immediate colleagues and line managers will react as well as the organisation as a whole.

» **The decision to identify with disability or ill-health was an 'emotional' transaction**

36%
suggest it is a big personal step to associate yourself with the word *disability*

27%
say some people resist the label because *"it feels so negaitve"*

52%
of all respondents knew the definition of disability in the Equality Act before sharing information

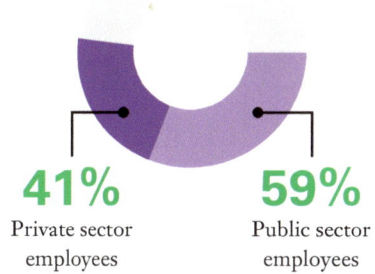

41% Private sector employees

59% Public sector employees

The respondents took considerable care to answer the survey offering detailed information about their experiences and ideas about how employers can better engage with them in terms of monitoring diversity data as well as creating a culture of confidence.

The four key themes included:

- Being clear about the purpose of monitoring

"I want my organisation to do something with the information it collects – if they are not going to do anything with the information, then I don't want to waste my time."

"Explain it from a company perspective – we can read the legal definition elsewhere – put it in the context of the culture, behaviours and values of the organisation."

"I have worked here for 15 years and answered many surveys – whether they are anonymous or not, I will never share information about my disability. I know how to manage it and know how to get by. I don't want pity and I don't need an adjustment so what is the point?"

- Focus on the culture, not the numbers

"The business should create the climate which makes people feel more empowered to disclose. This includes having role models, a disability network and visible success factors."

"Spend time celebrating everyone's differences…This makes it more comfortable for people to share their personal information if they have trust."

- Offer imaginative and authentic leadership

"Have leaders that are open about the fact that we all have personal difficulties one way or another – and it is OK to need help. The stereotype image of 'strong/no struggles here leadership' makes some of us feel hugely inadequate."

- Provide clear sign-posting to get more advice

"Have a knowledgeable advice team who can provide accurate and practical information to employees, managers and colleagues."

"Have a diversity passport (or workplace adjustment agreement template) which can be adapted and taken from role to role with details of disability and reasonable adjustments."

"Managers can't be expected to know what every disability is and what the adjustments might be for different people. My disabilities are not visible but have been life changing. We need to support those who acquire a disability to get the support they need and to line managers to be the helpful hustlers. But we shouldn't have to train everyone – it is just about first-class signposting and systems.

Views of employers

We asked our 55 employer partners about their existing practices about how and when they ask their employees whether they have a disability or not whether they formally monitor, and what their challenges are in this area.

There were many reasons why the employers wanted to get involved in the project:

"We are keen to tackle the stigma around mental health and being able to talk about it in the workplace with no fear of being stigmatised."

"We want to see what the current marketplace trends are for this area of work. To hear what other employers are doing. No-one has tackled this issue and so we all struggle."

"We want ideas about how we can improve our processes and are keen to hear what others are doing in this area – should we start with monitoring or just get on with plans."

"This is a topic we have discussed a lot and have never come to the 'right' answer!"

The key driver in monitoring

The employer participants all expressed an ongoing desire to better understand the issues that disabled employees face at work as part of building an inclusive workplace. The majority focused on the workplace adjustment process as a key driver in wanting better data. Some employers suggested that it is hard to justify improvement exercises to the adjustment process without accurate data about the number of disabled people employed by the organisation. Others wanted to create parity with the other protected characteristics, in monitoring data about pay, progression, reward, promotion, training and were exploring how to incorporate disability into existing data capture exercises.

Prevalence of monitoring and levels of accuracy

Among the employers surveyed, knowledge about the number of disabled employees as a proportion of the total workforce is mixed. The type of data collected also varies.

In response to the question 'do you formally monitor the number of disabled employees that you have' 73% of the 55 employers answered yes.

73%

of the 55 employers surveyed formally monitor the number of disabled employees they employ

34%

of the 55 employers surveyed did not know how many disabled employees they employed

Yet when asked how many disabled employees were employed 34% said they did not know how many disabled employees they employed. Some said the discrepancy between anonymous and non-anonymous surveys was so significant it meant that the data was unreliable and meaningless. Many employers cited how hard it was to collect information, particularly from those employees who may have acquired an impairment while at work.

Other data monitored

83% of the 55 employers monitor the number of new disabled entrants. This data is captured after job offer and onboarding though as part of a general induction and familiarisation programme with new recruits in order to offer any adjustments that may be needed.

While many employers are keen to improve the workplace adjustment process only 42% of the 55 employers monitor the number of adjustments provided. Moreover only 18% of the 55 monitor data about the speed and quality of adjustments made.

While nearly all employer participants engaged with the key questions and topics of debate that the report pose, 76% of the 55 employers sometimes use the language of 'declaration' and 'disclosure' in written communication or in discussion.

Employers struggle to decide how to phrase the definition of disability when monitoring. 96% surveyed use the definition used within the Equality Act. 31% supplement the definition of disability with examples of people who might be covered by the definition and use examples of people with different impairments. Global organisations struggle the most choosing to use the UN definition supplemented by local, legal definitions.

The key challenges

Employers acknowledge that while a monitoring exercise might be seen as transactional for the employer, it is often personal and emotional for the employee. Employers acknowledge that this is the case in both formal monitoring exercises and at other times when colleagues share information about their disability. This is a key challenge for employers.

The employers surveyed expressed their need to improve their data capture but want to do this by better reflecting that they understand this key dynamic. Many feel constrained by structural and procedural systems that do not allow for imaginative and 'human' communication methods. One or two employers expressed disappointment in their legal teams; having to balance a strategic imperative to communicate that the business wants to do well by its people with the risk of non-compliance in delivering workplace adjustments.

The purpose of data capture

The employers surveyed recognised that language can often get in the way of building an accurate picture about their workforce. The vast majority are keen to find new approaches to make it easier for people to share information about their disability and to respond in appropriate ways. Employers suggested that there are two key reasons why they want better data. Firstly, to create better plans in order to reduce barriers for groups

---

While many employers are keen to improve the workplace adjustment process only 42% of the 55 employers monitor the number of adjustments provided

42%

18%

Moreover, only 18% monitor data about the speed and quality of adjustments made

While nearly all employer participants engaged with the key questions and topics of debate that the report pose,

76%

of the 55 employers use the language of 'declaration' and 'disclosure'

96%

surveyed use the definition used within the Equality Act

31%

supplement the definition of disability with examples of people who might be covered by the definition and used examples of people with different impairments

of people at a business (macro) level. Secondly, to create better processes to make specific adjustments at the individual (micro) level.

Employers recognise the need to be clearer about specifying the limits to which they will use/pass on information that is given in monitoring processes and to specify why they asking for information and in what context. Most of the employers also suggested that they need to get better at signposting individuals to information about what adjustments they can get, and how to do so. 75% of the employers expressed concern about whether their processes (to data capture) were 'joined up' or consistent.

Of those surveyed 63% have a centralised workplace adjustment process. 38% have a centralised budget for workplace adjustments. 43% used a Disability Passport or Tailored Adjustment Agreement such as the one developed by Business Disability Forum.

Employers expressed again and again their wish to convey the message that disability and ill-health are normal life events and that they want to start with the principle that they are likely to be able to make an adjustment (which both parties will want to be reasonable – or which 'feels fair'). Employer participants often expressed that, when they do ask for information, they do not want to convey the impression that the employer believes 'having a disability makes you fragile' or that 'all disabled people need adjustments'.

75%

of the employers expressed concern about whether their processes (to data capture) were 'joined up' or consistent

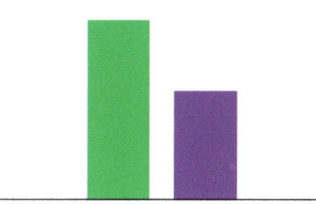

Of those surveyed
63%
have a centralised workplace adjustment process.
38%
have a centralised budget for workplace adjustments

> "We should be much more vocal and visible on our own company websites about the support we give to our disabled staff – the existence of networks – so from day one they are not embarrassed to enquire about or request adjustments and support – this should be part of our mainstream message not an add-on in one-off campaigns."

> "If you can't educate all the line managers then go for the education of people with a disability so they can help their line manager with what to do."

> "Celebrate senior disabled people's successes within the organisation and regularly include articles on this in corporate newsletters."

> "Make it explicit that requesting an adjustment will not have a detrimental effect on the career of disabled employees."

> "Let employees self-refer so they have control over the decision to share information or not."

> "Make sure that company stories, town-halls, newsletters have lots of stories of successful disabled employees. And doubly make sure the stories don't just focus on the adjustments that has been made, that's just good housekeeping – focus on how brilliant they are and what they do for the business."

[SECTION THREE]

15 BIG IDEAS
…for employers to try

"Some rules are nothing but old habits that people are afraid to change"
—*Terese Anne Fowler, Souvenir*

This section offers 15 big ideas for employers. Using the findings from the research, we bust some of the myths that employers have about monitoring and data capture.

It also touches on the broader experiences of disabled employees at work. The 15 big ideas are for employers to discuss, debate, to try out for size, to build on or throw out. Our intent is to get us thinking a bit more deeply about how to develop world-class engagement strategies.

We think that there is something here for every organisation, irrespective of how far down the journey they are, what size the organisation is or what sector they operate in. Some of the ideas will be old ones for some, and might seem like a step too far for others. Just think of them as ideas to mull on, discuss in Diversity and Inclusion teams, consider at executive level and debate with employees.

[1] Your organisation is not different

If you get low responses to surveys on disability and think it is about the 'sector' you work in, or type of 'trade' you work in, or 'fear of job security' or size of your organisation, think again.

It is easy to fall into the trap of assuming that the reasons for low responses are linked to factors you have no control over: sector, trade, size of organisation, economic climate or downsizing.

However our findings suggest that the decision about whether to share information about disability is not *primarily* about any of these things. While they may have a part to play, the reasons why people find it hard to share information about disability or ill-health are more likely to be found elsewhere.

Some of the reasons people keep quiet about disability (if they can) are about cumbersome self-service systems. Some reasons are about organisations poorly communicating why they need to know. And some of the reasons run far deeper – workplaces are not separate from society and the debate on disability more generally.

We found no significant correlation between employers who have better levels of data (that is, numbers that are closer to national statistics) and certain types of industry or types of employer.

Disability, injury and ill-health happen in every business and we can and should all adapt to it. Who knows when circumstances will affect us, and with an ageing workforce we need to get creative and work around challenges, not ignore them and hope they will go away.

[2] Help your people to manage a journey

One of the key findings from the 2,511 survey respondents is that their decision to share information about disability or ill-health is often related to the individual journey of understanding and making sense of disability/ill-health and then mapping that experience against the known track record of the organisation.

The indicators that people use in deciding whether to share information include:
- the ease by which the organisation provides information about workplace adjustments,
- the ease by which people can navigate the process and secure the adjustment and
- the skill with which the organisation celebrates human difference and specifically disabled talent.

Our findings suggest that the promotion of successful case studies about internal disabled talent is one of the most important drivers in cultural change. That might include ensuring that there are opportunities for role models and particularly senior disabled employees to share their experience of difference, or stories on the organisation's website about the types of creative adjustments that have been provided and the business impact of doing that. Or it might include ways to demonstrate that corporate social responsibility policies take account of the need to partner with rights-based organisations not just those that alleviate suffering in health and social care.

Helping people to manage a journey is critical and has direct impact on an individual's decision to share information, or not.

[3] Know what you can measure

> *"Not everything that counts can be counted, and not everything that can be counted counts."*—Albert Einstein

The amount of time and money spent in collecting accurate data about the number of disabled employees should not come at the expense of improving the workplace adjustment process and the lived experience of disabled employees.

Albert Einstein's great breakthrough came when he put known measures to one side. He realised that philosophical steps must be taken if breakthroughs were to be made.

There are no quick and simple ways to improve data levels. We are often asked to provide "the one question" that will result in accurate data.

Guess what? There isn't one. Building more accurate data is part of a process.

Moreover a better process alone will do nothing without better efforts to build disability confidence among employees and more widely across the organisation.

Among those employers that have improved the rate by which individuals share information, there are a number of things going on. They include targeted and imaginative campaigns encouraging people to share information. These campaigns always start with well-thought-through explanations as to why the organisation would like the information and what they will do as a result as well as a timeline by which feedback on future plans will be provided.

However, the fact is that it is not possible to obtain wholly accurate numbers about the number of disabled employees. The good news is that it is possible to improve the lived experience of disabled employees without them. The latter is not contingent on the former unless the employer is fixated on data in order to start working on the quality of that experience. But you don't need numbers to change experiences.

A word of caution, if employers are outsourcing the monitoring process or outsourcing the production and analysis of staff surveys to external organisations and consultancies they would be wise to test the credibility of understanding when it comes to the dynamics of disability.

[4] Learn from 'standout' integrated campaigns

We did come across some 'standout' campaigns in relation to data capture during the course of the project. These campaigns have been designed to support employees to feel more comfortable in sharing information about disability. Two of these campaigns come from BT and the Civil Service which we examine in our Case Study section (section five).

Both took a similar 'integrated' approach in their work to increase the level of data and thought about the things they have needed to do *in advance* of the campaign. Both demonstrate the need for 'systems-thinking' in the design of the campaign and the need to explain, in depth the purpose in wanting to improve levels of data.

However, neither started from the premise that plans to improve the experience of disabled employees would await the data.

These, and the other campaigns that we came across which were designed to improve data capture, seemed to combine four things.
- They thought deeply about purpose;
- They often used 'light-touch' user-friendly language;
- They signposted people to the workplace adjustment process or got in touch with them;
- They are investing in the improvement of the process by which people can share experiences about how to get ahead at work.

[5] Use external sources of data

While it is hard to get accurate data we step back from recommending that employers don't bother.

One of the main drawbacks in not conducting monitoring exercises is that it reduces one avenue for building a more accurate picture about workforce composition, especially when such data might be helpful to

> » **It is not possible to obtain wholly accurate numbers about the number of disabled employees. The good news is that it is possible to improve the lived experience of disabled employees without them**

improve financial forecasting and planning assumptions with regard to workplace adjustments.

Our view is that if employers don't have accurate data, and/or fail to secure reliable internal data, and the cultural norm is to plan for activities on the basis of data alone, then they should look to the external sources of data that might tell them more about the prevalence of disability or ill-health at work.

Employers may wish to use external sources of statistics to plan activities to improve the experiences of disabled employees such as those provided by the Labour Force Survey or the Office for National Statistics. We recommend that employers use this basic data in the absence of internal management information to benchmark trends.

[6] Bring different sources of data together

Employers must think carefully about asking questions about disability of their employees. If employers do not have the time, nor the inclination to think deeply about these things, it is probably better if they don't ask at all. Crucially, employers need to be clear about their reason for monitoring and how the data will be used.

There are different levels and layers of sharing information at the macro (organisational monitoring process level) and micro (requesting adjustments and telling colleagues level) and your data capture will be partly determined on how you describe the purpose of the first and make it easier for people to do the latter.

Just because it cannot be done with 100% reliability it is not wrong to try. Done with care, it can be a helpful method of understanding where you are with disability. The key is to focus on having a centralised and/or end-to-end workplace adjustment process.

In addition one-off initiatives to improve data gathering are unlikely to be wildly successful unless it chimes with other 'positive' initiatives that demonstrate the organisation wants to invest in its disabled talent and support their career development.

Employers may also do well by creating a composite picture of the workforce by bringing together different forms of data capture such as those who request workplace adjustments, facilities management information (e.g. the number of adaptations requested) anonymous employee engagement surveys, absence management data, occupational health data and the number of people who join a network.

[7] Don't start with data, build a route-map

> *"Happiness is like a butterfly: the more you chase it, the more it will elude you. But if you turn your attention to other things, it will come and sit softly on your shoulder."*—Thoreau

Of those employers that are doing well in collating more accurate figures about their disabled employees, they tend to have the following in common:
- They don't waste time collecting data to the detriment of reviewing the experiences of their disabled employees;

> » **If employers do not have the time, nor the inclination to think deeply about these things, it is probably better if they don't ask at all**

- They adopt systematic planning processes to improve the experiences of their disabled employees;
- They have senior business leaders who encourage the discipline of 'review and improve' over time and they bed the process into 'business as usual';
- They have a solid track record in mapping their journey of 'disability confidence' and benchmark their performance;
- They deliver consistent messages about the value they place in their disabled employees and invest in specific programmes to support their career development;
- They invest in their disability networks/resource groups and create specific initiatives that support people to build confidence, resilience and career goals.

In a nutshell, they start somewhere else than with the need for data and build a route-map for how they can improve the lived experience for disabled employees. And this gets them better data.

[8] Don't get bogged down in definition

There is only so much you can do to make it easy for employees to understand the Equality Act's definition of disability and ill health. And our findings show that for some they will never share information with their employer.

In section five we offer case studies from BT and the Civil Service about how they have gone about the process of improving data capture and in section seven we offer some general tips about how to monitor.

Employers should think creatively about how they can maximise the opportunity for people to understand that this means "people like them" when they use the word 'disability'. However our advice is not get bogged down with this. This is all about how people can be themselves and access the adjustments they need.

The legal definition was created for a particular purpose and the language of the courts is not the language of everyday life.

It is a crude instrument if used as a yardstick to determine how many disabled people you may have. It is a word which will, more often than not, be seen as a pejorative term and there is nothing the legislators or disability-rights campaigners can do about it. Every day there are new people who fit the definition but many may not know it. The social model taught us much about the real causes of human barriers way beyond physical, or neurological, or sensory or mental function but we have forever grappled with the fact that the new entrants are on a journey of understanding.

Our advice is that employers make it easier for employees to know that you mean people with diabetes, cancer, facial disfigurement, dyslexia, polio, back pain, RSI and many others when you talk generally about disabled people.

Time spent debating the definition of the term "disability" and what constitutes a "disability" is ultimately a diversion of time which could be better spent influencing people and making positive change. The words you use are important but should be broad enough to include people who don't consider themselves to be disabled. This is not about forcing people to identify with the word 'disability'.

Defining disability and knowing 'how many you have' in your organisation is NOT the destination. You will never get there. It is only a part of the journey towards disability confidence and effective inclusive working practices that allow everyone to give of their best. Don't make it a long detour.

[9] Get over "Chair envy"

From time to time we come across employers who share fears about the potential unintended consequences that might come from making the workplace adjustment process widely available, easy to access and easy to use. One such consequence could be that the employer might be subject to multiple requests from people who might "want" adjustments rather than "need" adjustments.

For the sake of illustrating this we might refer to this as "chair envy", where someone with a genuine back condition, considered disabled under the Equality Act and who has been provided with a suitable chair to help them be productive and effective, triggers a wave of requests from others who would similarly like a 'fancy chair'.

We asked three experts their views about how employers can avoid abuse of workplace adjustment systems. Here is what they said:

> **Expert opinion**
>
> "If your process for assessing need is robust then people shouldn't be able to 'swing the lead.' If they can, it's the process that is flawed.'" —**Phil Friend, Phil & Friends**
>
> "When employers have a robust centralised process with experienced people assessing need, you reduce the likelihood of abuse. It's much easier to abuse a fragmented process where there is no consistency or oversight." —**Nasser Siabi, Chief Executive, Microlink**
>
> "One of the best processes we have seen is that developed by Lloyds Banking Group – their systems-led approach, quality guidance for colleagues and line managers and routine follow-up is providing a consistent approach that our members and partners are following." —**Susan Scott Parker, Chief Executive, Business Disability Forum**

Our best advice is to get real. Don't miss the chance to do the right thing just because someone else might try to take advantage. All systems are open to abuse. The good criminal justice system errs on the basis that it is better that one guilty criminal escape justice than that an innocent person be condemned. The best adjustments system will be founded on a similar principle.

> **Treating people fairly sometimes means treating people differently**

[10] Don't 'disclose' or 'declare': share

You wouldn't use inappropriate language in your marketing material, why use it in your monitoring material? If the aim is to offer formal invitations to employees to contribute to an impersonal data collection exercise then it is best to use neutral language that chimes with intent. Repeated use of the terms 'disclosure' or 'declaration' might have a detrimental impact on how disabled employees view the integrity of an organisation's assertion of being disability confident.

Having a disability or health condition should not be linked to something akin to a secret or a big piece of news. Employers, within the constraints of time and resource might do well to support line managers to understand the importance of language here.

Of course for some employees, who may have a new disability, it may well feel like a secret or a big piece of news but employers can make this a bit easier. The legalese of 'disclosure' or 'declaration' compounds the fear that you may have to prove your right to support or adjustments – not a prospect that appeals to many of us.

Our advice is don't use these words in any of your written materials and avoid, if possible using the expressions informally in teams and action groups. Instead you could talk about 'sharing relevant information about your disability, health condition, illness or injury', or 'sharing information'. Even if the language of 'disclosure' is used by disabled people and people with a health condition themselves, using it is demeaning us all.

This is all about encouraging people to be themselves at work, and to share relevant information that employers can use in practical ways to drive positive change. Managers do not need to be medical experts so anything an employer can do to keep the subject in the sphere of 'what is relevant' the better.

These things may seem trivial especially when there are significant deliverables in the diversity and inclusion space but language matters. If you want an easy life, then best move out of diversity and inclusion.

Ditch the language of 'disclosure' and 'declaration' and adopt that of enabling performance. Organisations routinely invest in the process of identifying learning and development needs in order to deliver training to equip staff. Why not think of the process by which people share information about their disability and adjustment in the same way? We wouldn't ask people to 'declare' their training needs, would we?

[11] Understand the space between dignity and need

There is no one universal definition of 'disability' in the UK and thankfully the old language of implying there is a national "register" is long gone.

However, some employees will have to juggle a number of different definitions with different criteria including the Access to Work system, eligibility to the Blue Badge parking scheme, exemptions from on-going prescription costs, eligibility to the Disabled Persons Railcard, eligibility to the Personal Independence Payment and even private schemes to make things easier in relation to air travel for example.

In work, as in other areas of life, treating people fairly sometimes means treating people differently. One of the greatest challenges we face today is how we collectively navigate new paths to preserve individual dignity while assessing means to fund the extra costs of disability.

In order for some people to play a full and active role in the UK society and to reach a level playing field that many of us might take for granted, it may sometimes necessary for people to be asked to demonstrate the things they cannot do. But this is directly opposite to what most human beings find comfortable and humane and often at odds with how employees want their colleagues to view them at work. It is still possible for employees to be themselves at work, be their best and need an adjustment.

[12] Find your home-grown change-agents

Andrew McDonald, one of the most senior disabled civil servants in Whitehall has made numerous speeches about the process of making sense of disability and the length of time it takes to adjust to new identities that often (though not always) come with disability. He has spoken openly about his experience of Parkinson's disease and cancer. At the end of March 2014 he stood down as chief executive of the Independent Parliamentary Standards Authority having been told that his cancer is incurable.

He often refers to the phrase "this Land is Our Land" and reminds audiences how people perform best when they are themselves, when they do not need to mask their experience, when they can be who they are, when the environment can be normalised for them and when they can secure the adjustments they need.

This authenticity about the experience of disability is one of the most critical components to driving change. A disabled employee is often best-placed to provide the blend of continual support and occasional challenge that will help another disabled worker on their own journey. Spotting the individual disabled change-agents within an organisation and creating the means by which they can support other people has in our view been completely under-rated. Spot the story-tellers inside your own organisation: they can often change hearts and minds far more effectively than those from outside.

We applaud his work; the impact is significant.

[13] Encourage people to be themselves

During the course of the Secrets & Big News project, Kate Nash Associates approached Richard Tyrie, CEO at GoodPeople,[8] a social enterprise that harnesses the talents and skills of diverse communities to create positive and social impact. We asked him: how can we help disabled people across organisations and industries to connect and support each other?

He suggested the Advisory Board examine the It Gets Better[9] campaign conceived by Dan Savage and his husband Terry Miller. The campaign is designed to inspire hope for young people who are lesbian, gay, bisexual or transgender who experience harassment and particularly those who may be experiencing significant distress or suicidal thoughts.

A key component of the campaign is the constant message that "it gets better" delivered by lesbian, gay, bisexual and transgender people themselves. The campaign works by people uploading videos about themselves and by sharing messages about their journey they share the universal truth that, over time, things gets better.

> » **Spot the story-tellers inside your own organisation**

> Our advice is to ditch the word 'reasonable' at the front end when referring to the adjustment process

There are 50,000 user-created videos as a result which have been viewed over 50 million times.

The Advisory Board asked themselves what would be the equivalent for disabled people at work. As a result, Andy Kneen at Shell conceived the Be Yourself campaign at Shell. The Case Study is cited in section five.

Our advice to employers is to notice the powerful role you can play when you enable people to be themselves at work – and in turn encouraging each other. Only they know the journey they go through and are often the people that are best placed to support others who feel nervous about sharing information which is often the first step in securing an adjustment if one is needed at all.

Encouraging people to Be Themselves is a powerful message to roll out.

[14] Remove 'reasonable' from the neon lights

The concept of reasonableness should underpin a workplace adjustment process but the word 'reasonable' doesn't need to be in the title of the policy or name of the process. It belongs at the back end with all the cogs and nuts and bolts.

The quality of your adjustments process is likely to be used as a personal yardstick to determine whether to share information about disability. If the process becomes more visible, easier to use and more efficient and effective for both soft adjustments for example to working hours, or for harder adjustments such as new equipment, this will be an important factor in improving rates by which people share information.

Our findings show that the majority of employers refer to the adjustment process as the 'reasonable adjustment process' in their policies, procedures and communications. As we have said, the concept remains a helpful legal one when the employer 'machine' considers its ability to make the adjustments for people, taking cost, disruption and health and safety into account. However our advice is to ditch the word 'reasonable' at the front end when referring to the adjustment process – simply refer to the 'workplace adjustment process'.

This simple change that is unlikely to cost anything other than some time, could have a major impact on people's willingness to share information and seek the adjustments they need.

[15] Think global, act local

For those employers who operate at a global level the definition of disability brings further challenges and opportunities. Most of the private sector organisations who contributed to this study operate in global markets where certain countries (Europe, North America) for different cultural and/or religious and/or other reasons, are likely to be more disability confident than other geographies (Asia, Africa).

While using the UN definition may be an option for employers wanting to harmonise multiple definitions when monitoring across country boundaries, it seems logical to share the 14 ideas above with colleagues globally.

[SECTION FOUR]

15 BIG IDEAS
…for disabled employees to try

> "It's not what you say out of your mouth that determines your life, it's what you whisper to yourself that has the most power"
> —*Robert T Kryosaki*

This section offers 15 big ideas for employees. As for the employers' section, we use the findings from the research to bust some of the myths that employees might believe. This time about sharing information about our disability or ill-health at work.

The 15 big ideas are for to get you thinking more deeply – discuss them, debate them. We think that there is something here for everyone, irrespective of their disability or impairment and how far down the journey they are in making sense of it. Just think of them as ideas to mull on, discuss in networks and with colleagues and managers.

[1] Don't prejudge monitoring
Stonewall produced a great booklet called 'What's It Got To Do With You?'[10] It explains why data on disability, age, gender, sexual orientation and belief may now be requested by employers and service providers, and what the benefit is. With many organisations responding to new measures in the Equality Act, 'What's it got to do with you?' makes the case for monitoring across all equality strands.

It is a great publication and provokes us all to 'get over ourselves' when considering whether to share information.

We think that the more disabled people feel able to share information in formal and informal ways the more able an organisation is to secure data that supports the case for change – in terms of pay, reward, progression etc. Sometimes we have to share factual information (e.g. I need to have a parking space because I can't use public transport or I need a loop or I won't hear anything in this seminar).

Of course these things are not always easy to do and for some of us we need a supportive environment before we chose to share information in the same way as we do our nationality or marital status for example.

But if we can get used to the idea of sharing information at work then we are more likely to help our employers build more confident systems to support people into work and stay there. This is a two-way deal – we have to play our part in the system before we can expect it to respond.

[2] Take your time

Most people who have had a disability for a long time will have a basic understanding of the Equality Act and how it is there to protect them, but understanding how it works is often more complex for people who are new to the experience of ill-health or disability. This applies to the individuals affected and their manager or colleagues.

Developing personal strategies for making sense of disability and ill-health and feeling able, when it is relevant, to share such information with our colleagues or line managers or the organisation more generally takes some of us a long time.

Naturally it can also be hard for our managers and colleagues to work out what to say, when to say it, how to help, when to ignore it. Acquiring a disability is a life-changing event and not just for those who acquire it.

Our survey respondents said again and again that it can take a bit of getting used to being 'different' and to learn how to manage our impairment whether we already had it when we started work with our organisation, or developed it along the way. And many of us, even those of us 'out, loud and proud' are forever learning new ways of being who we are at work.

This may appear to make it more challenging for all parties but there is no right or wrong way. We are forever learning. There is no "one size fits all" approach – but of course it helps to have a supportive environment to help people manage this change.

[3] Don't let definition be a barrier

It's important you know the law. But your experience of living with ill-health or disability while still doing your job brilliantly is so much more important.

For some people who have an impairment that is obvious. They may not be too fussed about sharing information because 'it's out there'. However, as we know, many health conditions that are disabling at work are not visible at all until we start to undertake a work activity and have some difficulties.

The trick is to not get hung up on definition. All employers grapple with the limitations of the definition of disability as expressed in the Equality Act. But that is a particular definition for a particular purpose.

The employers that monitor do so within strict parameters regarding what they do with the information.

The employers who took part in our survey, and who monitor, would prefer employees with a disability to share information so they can become more aware of the needs of their workforce, make better planning decisions and action accordingly. We didn't come across any who were building up a hit list of folk to fire. Honest.

[4] Don't be defined

One of the things that came up in our survey was the fear that sharing information about ill-health or disability would end up defining who we are. This does not need to be the case. Of course for many people the experience can be a fundamental part of who we are and can have a major impact on how we do things but it does not need to define us.

Naturally you will come across people who you work with who might get a bit "stuck" and cannot see past your experience of ill-health or disability. Practice makes perfect when it comes to this.

Certainly having a few one-liners up your sleeve can be helpful. Tom, who has Asperger's Syndrome, works in a company of 70,000 employees. Sometimes he is asked if he knows the telephone extension of all 70,000 of his colleagues off by heart. Sometimes he explains that everyone is different including different people with Asperger's. Sometimes he says yes.

At the end of the day human beings are curious. It can get a little tiring to have to repeatedly explain things but disability need not define you unless you wish it do so. And that is ok too but allowing ourselves to be defined by any one thing can seriously limit our capacity for change both in our work and in our personal development.

[5] Talk to other disabled employees

> "Life is 10 percent what you make it and 90 percent how you take it."
> —Irving Berlin

Anyone who has lived with a health condition, illness or disability that has affected their ability to do their job to the best of their ability will have something to share – even if it feels like it is unlikely to be useful.

In our work with networks and resource groups we come across too many folk who think that people with different impairments have nothing in common. Being able to make the connections about the things people have in common is the thing that enables networks to flourish and become vibrant change-mechanisms. Indeed, the ability to make the sorts of connections that are not obvious is a key skill in many jobs too. We share the common denominator of how we can remain productive and good at our jobs at same time as managing difference and asking for adjustments.

For example, in many ways someone's experience of deafness will be different to someone with a degenerative neurological condition. And someone else with a visual impairment may have little practical advice to offer about helpful adjustments to someone with arthritis but dig a little deeper. The reality is far different.

All these people want to be themselves at work. Talking to others who feel this way is one of the most liberating ways to build resilience. Networking also enables you to gain tips and advice about managing an impairment while delivering the day job.

We are not talking about the sloppy stuff – we are talking about the tough stuff. How you build resilience? How you get a mentor? How you gear yourself up for a conversation that your line manager may not be expecting? You can think of more.

Networking with other disabled employees, irrespective of the type or severity of their impairment or how long they have had it can yield really useful advice about how to get ahead at work and sometimes push you to think more positively – and even differently – about your career prospects. It can be one of the most powerful things you can do.

> **It can get a little tiring to have to repeatedly explain things but disability need not define you unless you wish it do so**

[6] Enjoy the journey

"Though the road's been rocky it sure feels good to me."—Bob Marley

Disability and ill health are not trivial.

It can be enormously hard for people to get through distressing times when the future looks bleak, or when people have to manage trauma, pain or ill health that affects life expectancy. Our work with many thousands of disabled people in work tells us that the crossroads between making sense of the future while managing the 'here and now' at work is anything but easy.

But our experience also tells us that there is a process of 'assimilation' of what it means to have a disability and a journey of understanding that many disabled people go through. The journey can last months, years or a lifetime. Where someone is on the journey will have an impact on what they want to share and what they don't, as well as with whom. This process is a normal part of the experience of disability and ill-health. This is not about the ability to 'cope' or not or 'come to terms with' something or not, it is about a natural cycle of understanding, applying that understanding and adding to it over time.

We hear again and again and again people referring to the things that they have learned along the way – about themselves, about others, about how the experience helps to focus the mind on life-goals and how it enhances understanding of what it means to be human. In other words, the journey can be a blast. Not always, and not for everyone, but it's just an idea that doesn't get much airtime.

[7] Be yourself – it gets easier

Being different is what makes life interesting. But being able to feel confident and comfortable in sharing information about disability and ill-health can take a bit of getting used to.

One of our survey respondents summed this up quite nicely:

"Sharing personal information is a bit like trying on new clothes – you need to practice. You need to practice talking about it when it is relevant to do so and especially when you are working with colleagues who might need to do things a bit differently in order for you to deliver your bit."

Our advice is to open up conversations with others. Debate the subject of sharing information with other colleagues. The more you can be yourself at work the more likely it is you will flourish and exude confidence and that in turn will help others feel confident in you. In section three (idea number 12) we invite employers to support this process.

It is not always easy to do this especially if you are struggling with sadness or depression. But for many, things do get better when we can be ourselves at work. In section five we offer a number of employer case studies – the Be Yourself campaign promoted by Shell may be of interest.

[8] Don't get hung up on disclosure

"The optimist sees the donut, the pessimist sees the hole."—Oscar Wilde

There is a school of thought tucked within social psychology that you get what you expect in life.

As one life coach says "your energy flows where your attention flows."

It is an interesting idea to mull on when considering the anxiety that many people have in relation to thinking about whether to share information or not. If we get the things we focus on, and we focus on not sharing information does that mean we get a bit stuck in thinking we have some kind of secret when we have a disability or health condition?

[9] Rehearse for 'chair-envy'

In the section three we encourage employers to develop good policies to make the workplace adjustment process easier to access and use. One consequence may be that the employer gets requests from people who "want" adjustments rather than "need" them. We called this "chair envy" where someone with a genuine back condition, who has been provided with a suitable chair to help them be productive and effective, triggers a wave of requests from others who would also like a new chair.

Sometimes being the recipient of a workplace adjustment means having to navigate your way through conversations with colleagues who want to know why you are doing things a bit differently. Whether that is flexibility about working hours or some whizz-bang technology or indeed a seemingly extravagant chair, you may from time-to-time be drawn into conversation. In order to survive and flourish at work, it may be an idea to rehearse the best way of explaining without feeling you have to, or indeed having to apologise either.

[10] Network

There is huge value in getting involved in a network or resource group – and in encouraging colleagues to get involved, including colleagues who may not experience disability or ill-health personally. The chances are they will know someone with a disability among their family or friends as well as you.

Like most things in life, you get out what you put in so think about what you can contribute. Not all networks or resource groups provide a "service" as such, although some of them do.

One of their most valuable roles is in providing support and practical speedy advice about how to get the right adjustment. They can often also offer ideas about how you can navigate the human resisters in building more inclusive work environments. They can act as a safe haven, a connector and a powerhouse to get over self-limiting expectations. They are also a magnet for the 'change agents' building a fresh narrative when it comes to the career prospects of disabled people. This makes them vibrant places to be.

Don't let other people's perceptions about disability or ill-health get in the way of you seeking advice that can rarely be found elsewhere.

[11] Be disability confident

Being confident and comfortable with disability at work can depend on a range of things:

- how long you have had a disability;
- the impact of its onset;
- the prognosis;
- how it fluctuates;
- how friends, loved ones, colleagues, the greengrocer have reacted;
- how quickly you have learnt skills and tactics for protecting yourself against others and your own self-limiting beliefs;
- whether your organisation has particular cultural traits and/or is downsizing.

It also depends on the type of person you are, whether you are extravert or an introvert. It might also depend on whether you have had practice in managing life challenges.

We have said before that it is likely that any monitoring system will be inherently flawed when it comes to disability. It is one of the most complex of the protected characteristics that the Equality Act 2010 encompasses because it is hard to "own" the label.

Ultimately our advice is that if you lack confidence, do what you need to do to build it. That is sometimes the first step before you can ask for a workplace adjustment.

In section ten and appendix six we map out criteria as to what makes a disability confident employee. We strongly advise employees and networks to debate this and develop their own definition of what makes a disability confident employee. It is the clue to how employers can get the best from you. It is also the clue for how you get the best from work and life.

It is worth remembering too that we often teach what we need to learn – by debating the topic you are likely to support others.

> » We often teach what we need to learn

[12] Provide positive feedback

Providing positive feedback to your employer which deliberately focuses on the good things being done to provide adjustments is often the best way of inviting interest and stimulating the appetite to do even better in the future. In other words the *way* you provide feedback to your employer about the organisational journey of disability confidence is as important as *what* you feedback.

This is not about distorting difficult experiences, or not telling the truth when things get bad, or pretending everything is going well when it isn't. However it is a fact that we learn more from knowing what we do well (in order to replicate) than what we do less well (in order to avoid repeating).

People, teams and organisations often change when there is a shared assumption that they want to give of their best and do better. The old mantra that the world changes when you practice forgiveness and make it easier for it to do so by example is a fundamental and universal force.

[13] Don't apologise

While practicing the art of providing positive feedback, it is also important not to apologise for a living.

Many people who have a disability or health condition will have to explain a little bit about how they live and work, particularly when colleagues have to adapt how they work, communicate or interact with them.

The key is to practice what you share and how you share it. The more able you are to take control of the pace and content of what you share the better, otherwise people might start to own your story or make assumptions about your experience of disability or ill health.

However you do not need to apologise for a living or tolerate fools. Just focus on being the best you can be, get the adjustments you need (if you need any at all), invest in yourself, your resilience and your career.

[14] Avoid being an inspiration

Being your best might sometimes cause others to think that you are a bit of an inspiration. Some people who have impairments that are visible or profoundly challenge peoples' views of human difference, might be exposed to colleagues who think they are brave for simply getting up in the morning.

Most of us won't want to aspire to inspire. We might feel that would send our all sorts of weird messages about what it means to be different. But it might be an idea to recognise that some people might see it that way.

Our advice is to just be good at what you choose to do with your career. Some people will see you as an inspiration. Being "out there" means you might get labeled as one, it happens. If it does, make the most of the opportunity it presents. But it's probably best to develop a few skills to sidestep some of the unintended consequences when folk simply want to say "you are doing good" when they can't quite find the words to do so or when they come out all wrong.

When you have lived with the 'tough stuff' that many folk with a disability do, you build resilience. To see this as brave or an inspiration is a normal human reaction: people find it hard to imagine how they would react if they too had the same impairment. You will know from the ups and downs that most of us react in the same way, but in the end we pick ourselves up, dust ourselves down and get on with it. There are no alternatives.

That said, role models are important. Whilst we advocate a level playing field and support for employees to be authentic and bring their true self to work, it is often unavoidable that they become celebrated as role models and change agents. This can and should be a force for good. However, manage your own publicity so that your employer doesn't fall into the trap of tokenism. You don't have to be the "disability poster boy or girl" – but recognise you can contribute to the process of making it easier for other disabled people.

» **Focus on being the best you can be, get the adjustments you need, invest in yourself, your resilience and your career**

> **Expert opinion**
>
> "Having a disability and being told you are inspirational can be flattering. When you've not actually done anything exceptional; going to work, going shopping, eating a meal it can become patronising. It re-enforces low expectations. So I'm not keen on being called inspirational but I do like it if someone becomes 'inspired to do' something. So next time you are called inspirational for doing something mundane, ask the person what they're inspired to do, what changes and improvements will they now make as a result of meeting you?" —**Simon Minty, Sminty Ltd (Disability Training & Consultancy)**

[15] Consider brand purple

When we buy products we often get drawn to a brand. The art of brand creation is about tapping into deep desires and aspirations. Branding is about drawing people to something unique, special, 'stand-out' and seductive. Professional brand creators know that humans buy things for all kinds of reasons which are often tied up with how we are perceived, as much as the usefulness of the product. If you think about some of the most iconic brands – Apple, Coca-Cola, BMW – they conjure up images of a certain lifestyle and image. They create a feeling associated with the product.

People are not brands and the word disability is a hard one to work up a seductive brand. Look at the ways disability networks struggle to find the right words to name their network and convey their purpose. Try as they might, they are challenged in finding an attractive network brand that folk will break down doors to get involved with. In fact, there are so many networks that in trying to remove themselves from the 'dis' part of the word and focus on the 'ability' part that they end up doing neither in the process. The joke is on us.

During 2013 we started to see more use of the concept of the 'purple pound'. In a BBC Ouch news feature in January 2014[11] it was highlighted how the colour purple is increasingly being used by campaigners, charities and the government to refer to the spending power of disabled people. And while the reporter could not find any meaningful or symbolic significance to the colour purple the article was a helpful reminder that lots of 'movements' adopt a colour and often that colour has significance to the particular cause. Grey (or sometimes silver) describes the hair colour of older people and pink has been ironically adopted by the LGBT community. In addition the symbolism of the Rainbow is often used by the LGBT community to convey the spirit of intent behind inclusion. Who could have failed to notice the subtle, and not so subtle use of rainbow symbolism from Google and others during the Sochi 2014 winter olympics?

If one of the greatest needs for employers is to find an easy, no-fuss way of messaging the fact that they value disabled talent and make adjustments where necessary why not move round the mountain of language? Seriously, why not make it easy for everyone and find some simple ways to help people connect to the experience of disability or ill-health without forcing folk to sign-up to the word disability? That just won't happen. We might want employers to expand a bit on the definition of disability when it comes to monitoring (see section six where we offer ways they can do this) but might it be easier to find a better way of branding a complex range of criteria?

Could there be any merit in using the phrase purple talent? When our senior business leaders are on platforms conveying their wish to include people like us, might we consider making it easier for them to 'reach' out to us all without listing all the examples we cited in the beginning of this book?

Should we now create purple networks across the business and public sector? Who cares where the origin of the colour came from.

> » **Could there be merit in using the phrase purple talent?**

[SECTION FIVE]

CASE STUDIES

"How wonderful it is that nobody need wait a single moment before starting to improve the world"—*Anne Frank*

There were many examples of good and emerging good practice amongst the employer participants. Those that we have chosen to highlight are those that have been designed to make it easy…
- for employees to be themselves at work;
- for employees to understand the benefits of sharing diversity information;
- for employees to get the adjustments they need;
- for line managers to know what to do to help;
- for employees to navigate the awkward or repeated conversations about adjustments;
- for colleagues to network with each other and access training to help them identify steps they might wish to take to define goals and succeed at work.

Shell – Be Yourself

Shell has 90,000 employees who work in over 70 countries. Be Yourself[12] is an innovative and interactive approach to help disabled employees be themselves at work featuring a series of short films from 15 Shell employees with a disability, across different geographies, and with different impairments the shared message is about why it's important to be yourself at work.

The campaign was launched to coincide with the United Nations International Day of Persons with Disabilities on 3rd December 2013.

The issue
One of Shell's core values is that people work together best when all are able to be who they really are but it understands that many people, especially those who are living with a disability, find this hard to do.

The idea
Andy Kneen, HR Manager at Shell, examined the It Gets Better campaign (a video sharing platform to give hope to LGBT youth that life gets better when you can be who you are) and asked the question:, 'is there an equivalent for disabled employees?'

The driver
Working collaboratively, the four different enABLE networks (employee disability networks) within Shell in the UK, US, Canada and The Netherlands identified employees to be interviewed. *Be Yourself* was positioned as an opportunity for employees to tell their story, explain how they manage their impairment, and why it is important to *be yourself*.

The resources
The internal communications department filmed the stories, got them subtitled and edited. IT resources created a website to host the content.

Smaller organisations with limited budgets can do the same for less simply using personal phones and tablets to record the video message and then hosting the content either through an existing website, or through an existing external platform, such as You Tube. The cost need not be restrictive. Once there is agreement for the concept in principle, there is the opportunity to be creative and use technology savvy employees to help bring it to fruition.

Overcoming resistance
Shell has established disability networks in four countries but is a global business and has many countries at different stages of becoming disability confident. To break down barriers in some countries, Shell used global webcasts with its HR community to explain the principles behind the Be Yourself campaign.

What do employees say?
For Shell the Be Yourself platform has given employees the confidence to share information about their impairment for the first time. This has been achieved through the power of storytelling and drawing inspiration from other Shell employees talking about their experiences.

> "Sharing information let me be who I am. I'm bringing my whole self to work." —Jannifer Rios

> "Sharing information for me is a way to prevent barriers being formed. If people know what my limitations are they will work around them as well as I do, which is beneficial for both of us. My autism is part of who I am and has also produced positive things. I'm autistic like I'm Dutch, like I'm an engineer, like I'm tall – it's just part of me."—Diederik Weve, chair of enABLE (disability) network in the Netherlands

What does Shell say?
"To enable the company to win, we need to be attractive and inclusive to diverse talent, and that includes people with disabilities. This is all about helping people to perform better, about our leadership attributes of performance and authenticity, and about our core value of respect for people. So I say: 'just be yourself'."—Jorrit van der Togt, Executive Vice President for Human Resources Strategy and Internal Communications.

> » **Once there is agreement for the concept in principle, there is the opportunity to be creative and use technology savvy employees to help bring it to fruition**

BT – The Passport

The BT Passport was developed in 2006. It is a simple word document that can be downloaded from the intranet by every BT employee. The document enables any employee with a disability to fill it in, recording what their disability is, how it affects them at work, the adjustments required and those subsequently agreed with their manager.

The document is only kept by the individual and the manager – when the individual moves on, they can present it to their new manager; when the manager moves on, the individual can make it available, if necessary, to the incoming manager.

The issue
BT wanted to help managers and staff have open practical conversations about their disability or health condition, how it impacts on them at work and what adjustments have been agreed. More importantly, once they'd had the conversation, BT wanted to ensure employees did not have to have repeated conversations about prior agreements. They also wanted to ensure customer service levels were not negatively impacted.

The idea
An employee with bi-polar told the business about a workplace adjustment they had agreed with their manager. Whilst the employee knew she had to let her manager know if she was having difficulties and occasionally wasn't able to come to work, sometimes she simply couldn't face speaking to anyone. Between them, they agreed she would send a text to her manager to say she was having difficulties with the condition and was going to struggle to come into work that day; this allowed her manager to support the individual and manage the business requirements. Then, when she felt more able, she would give him a call. It's worth bearing in mind that this was 2006 and using a text to tell your boss you were unwell and couldn't come to work was fairly radical! Once the adjustment had been agreed, it worked really well but she realised if she changed jobs or her manager changed, she would have to start the conversations from scratch and that felt like too much unnecessary pressure.

The driver
When the employee came to the Diversity team, they immediately knew this was a common sense way of managing workplace adjustments. They set about creating the passport in collaboration with the Chief Medical Officer. They trialled it with a number of disability network members and subsequently made some minor enhancements to make it as user friendly as possible.

The resources
The Passport is a simple word document; there is no cost involved. The passport questions can be tailored to suit the organisation. It was branded as a "passport" to get people through the process of working with a new manager. It enables conversations to take place and questions about agreed

adjustments to be discussed as quickly as possible without fuss or repetition and therefore allowing people to feel supported, confident and more able to achieve their potential.

Overcoming resistance

Because this is such a simple, easily used tool there was no resistance to getting it set up as one of BT's tools to support people.

The deliverables

The passport has been embraced by many employees as a tool to manage conversations that are sometimes difficult and could be lengthy, even though adjustments have been agreed previously.

The passport is not kept centrally so the business does not know nor track the number of passports that are being used. Strong and positive feedback shows that where it is used, both the manager and the individual feel it is a helpful tool to map what adjustments have been or might need to be made.

The success of the Disability Passport has been used to create other passports for different situations. BT now has a Health & Wellbeing Passport, a Carer's Passport and are working on other passports to add to the Passport family. In addition Business Disability Forum have created the Tailored Adjustment Agreement.[13]

What do employees say?

The Disability Passport has become a highly valued tool to help disabled people and people with a health condition to 'frame' and 'retain' the agreed adjustments between the individual and the organisation. It enables employees to fast-track the "awkward" conversation and get on with their job without having repeated conversations.

> **"The disability passport is a one stop shop that saved me repeating myself about my condition to line managers. The passport captured in a concise manner all the relevant points about my condition how it affects me and how simple achievable things can stop flare ups."**

> **"I recently moved to a new role and I found the passport really helpful. It reminded me of the adjustments that I had come to take for granted."**

> **"It has been vital in helping line managers to best understand my disability, for them to recognise my coping strategies and for me to gain the support necessary to discharge a fully effective role in BT".**

What does BT say?

"The Disability Passport is a great example of the business and its people working together to create a practical solution to a challenging issue. With the Passport people feel more able to have a conversation with their managers about their disability or health condition which is good for our people and good for business."

BT – 'Count Me In' campaign

In late 2013 BT launched their "Count Me In" campaign. The campaign radiates the message that BT wants its people to share personal information in order to shape the business in the future. It made clear that an increase in reliable information would result in making better informed decisions about people issues. The campaign focused on the positive effects of having a better understanding of the make-up of the BT employee base. It provided an opportunity to restate the BT inclusion vision included everyone, actively encouraging and celebrating difference.

The issue
Employees at BT have historically been good at letting the business know their diversity information. At the end of the 2012–13, 75.1% of their people in the UK had told the business whether or not they had a disability. However of that number only 4.92% had said they had a disability or health condition.

BT felt significant numbers of people were not letting them know either because they didn't feel comfortable with how the information would be used, or that the information they provided wasn't going to be confidential.

BT had also fallen into the trap of using language that wasn't particularly inclusive or helpful; they used the words 'declaration' and 'disclosure' which, while in common usage by companies in the UK, conveyed a sense of "big brother" and suggested a disability or health condition was something to be kept hidden. BT wanted to do something about this.

The idea
BT worked with communications teams across the businesses and together they conceived of the "Count Me In" campaign. The premise is that if you make it easier for people to understand why a business wants information about protected characteristics and peoples' diversity data, the more able you are to dispel fears and concerns.

The driver
The campaign drivers come from the Inclusion team as well as people from other parts of the business. This integrated approach has helped BT get the message out to the maximum number of people. BT has nearly 75,000 people based in the UK and another 15,000 based globally. The campaign was supported by a senior inclusion sponsor, who made a personal commitment that the information was confidential and explained exactly how the information would be used.

The resources
The resource requirements for the campaign have been small. The challenge was in finding ways to reach the largest number of people, a significant number of whom were not office based i.e. the engineering workforce. The project team worked closely with the communications

teams across the businesses to find out the best way to tailor the generic communications for different parts of the business.

Benefits to employees and BT
At the point of going to press it is still early days to see how successful the campaign has been. BT has one simple success measure – have more of its people felt comfortable in sharing their diversity information? In just a few months, feedback has shown that people welcome a different approach from the business, the more transparent way it was asking for information and the explanations given on how the information would be used.

Civil Service – the value of sharing disability information

In 2013 Civil Service Departments joined forces pooling know-how and resources to create and roll out clear and simple information packs about the value of sharing diversity data. Government departments worked to a common aim – to get better data about the diversity of their people in order to improve planning and action.

The issue
Government departments want to embed diversity and inclusion into all aspects of their business. They want to make a difference to the experience of their people and reflect the society they serve. Benchmarking data enables departments to understand the make-up of their workforces and improve the coverage, consistency, quality and transparency of the employment equality data that is held. But employee response rates concerning disability status and other diversity information varied between departments, and were often lower than external and reputable bodies suggested.

The idea
The Civil Service-wide network group of Diversity leads (Heads of Diversity Group) commissioned a sub-group to make it easier for departments to improve the rates of data capture and find creative ways to encourage individuals to update their diversity information.

It became clear that line managers are a crucial enabler to support consistent messages about the value of good data and needed tools to support this. An information pack was designed for managers at all levels across the Civil Service.

The driver
The sub-group, acting on behalf of the Civil Service with the Chair providing overall guidance to complement individual internal strategies and activities drove the project from start to finish taking every opportunity to communicate news about the product,. Numerous groups and individuals at all levels were consulted across departments and agencies.

> **Trust was a major issue, with employees concerned about confidentiality and the potential negative impact on their careers**

The resources
The resources were mostly about taking the time to think deeply about the human and individual resisters to sharing diversity information and in this case, the challenge of sharing information about disability and ill health. Existing information was used to benchmark the current position across Government, including Office for National statistics figures and internal survey results from different departments.

Time was spent on understanding the ways response rates could be improved and ideas developed to encourage completion by different groups of employees.

Overcoming resistance
The sub-group was keen to address the need for clear and simple information about why this data was necessary from busy people working in government departments, many of which have experienced down-sizing in the last few years.

Three key needs were identified:
- Most departments gather workforce diversity data through voluntary updates to online HR systems – IT systems can be difficult and time consuming to access;
- Most senior leaders were reluctant to share information about ethnicity and disability status, and without them on board, it was difficult to get others to do so;
- Trust was a major issue, with employees concerned about confidentiality and the potential negative impact on their careers.

To build trust, positive encouragement not mandatory compliance was used as the key driver.

A lot of time was taken to talk to key stakeholders to explain the roll out of other plans that would improve the experience of disabled employees.

The deliverables
A one stop line managers' Information pack was introduced which explained the business case for diversity information, guidance and a Q&A brief which could be shared with employees and examples of best practice for encouraging colleagues to check their personal data is correct.[14]

What do employees say?
Understanding the composition of the workforce helps the Civil Service to highlight differences between groups in terms of satisfaction, engagement and representation, and will target actions that will improve the experience of disabled employees in all aspects of their working life.

What does the civil service say?
The resource pack has been shared with Diversity Practitioners and Heads of Diversity across the Civil Service. Employee advocate groups such as Employee Diversity Networks, including the Civil Service Disability Network, and the National trade unions were consulted. Views were also sought from individual disabled colleagues and line managers from across the Civil Service.

"This is really useful – it will help us improve the working conditions of people with disabilities."

"I only wish we'd done this sooner! This will help me to explain why we ask for this information and how we'll use it to help all our colleagues."

"I hope this is being promoted in every department."

Lloyds Banking Group – Systemic Grounds to Succeed

In 2000 a systemic approach to disability was put in place as part of Lloyds TSB's approach to Equality & Diversity. It created a route-map driven by less than 4 FTEs across approx 95,000 employees and over 30 million customers.

Driven by the core goal of building lasting relationships with customers Lloyds knew that this could only be done by representing the customers and the communities in which they live. In order to do this the business needed to be reflective of those communities, including people with disabilities.

The issue
Lloyds wanted to provide colleagues with the grounds to succeed in the organisation – to perform to their full potential and contribute to the success of Lloyds Banking Group.

The idea
The business, through key personnel, decided that systemic and long-term change would come from three mutually supporting swim-lanes within an overarching strategy:
- a formal adjustment process to create a level playing field;
- targeted development training to improve confidence and career prospects of disabled employees;
- a colleague network to provide mutual support.

The driver
Quality leadership in each swim-lane has been essential to maintain progress over time. Executive sponsors for each diversity strand were appointed in 2010 in order to drive business ownership of diversity. The Group Operations Director was appointed executive sponsor for disability. He brought three core qualities to the process:
- a practical, business focused approach – he "fixes things" and there were aspects of Lloyds approach to disability that needed fixing;
- an emphasis on getting the basics right;
- a determination to ensure that it becomes business as usual – it is embedded and becomes "how we do things round here."

A cultural driver was the shared understanding that getting processes right made good business sense: there is no point having people unable to perform to their full potential and no point losing people and having to recruit replacements.

A Group Disability Programme team of 2 was appointed which drew in stakeholders. For example a newly appointed network Chair and the Diversity & Inclusion team responsible for the personal development programmes. They all worked to a refreshed and common plan. Outcomes for each swim-lane were intensified:

Workplace adjustment process
The then workplace adjustment process was deemed unfit for purpose and plans were created for an overhaul. Three criteria were agreed:
- one size did not fit all (i.e. assessments should only be undertaken when needed and to fast track everything else);
- line managers should be involved but not drive the process (so not acting as a bottleneck);
- funding for adjustments should be centralised to eliminate local concerns over costs.

Personal Development and Career Development Programmes
These specialised programmes were reaffirmed as essential and funding was ring fenced to ensure their continuation. The executive sponsor saw the benefits of the investment made in this training going far wider than the colleagues receiving it – a pebble in the pond creating ripples of cultural change

The colleague network "Access"
The colleague network "Access" was relaunched with a mandate to be "the voice" of disabled colleagues and an active stakeholder in the delivery of improvements. This included the introduction of colleague support networks focused on specific conditions, a mentoring scheme, Assistive Technology User Group, development of regional networks and an events programme.

The resources
The programme team is staffed with less than 4 full-time equivalents.

This team then works with a range of functional leads – the principle being that improvements come by delivering through others. Lloyds Banking Group use the Disability Standard created by Business Disability Forum to spread disability confidence across the organisation by having a sponsor and workstream lead for each of the 10 DS criterion.

Lloyds believe the essential driver has been to secure an Executive Sponsor who owns the problems together with accountable resource to deliver fixes.

The deliverables
Workplace adjustments has now served over 17,000 colleagues since March 2010. The average rate is 150 cases per week. The average case

duration for fast-track cases is 3 days. For those needing assessment the average is 11 days.

The satisfaction rating of the workplace adjustment process from colleagues and line managers is 85% happy/very happy.

The Personal and Career Development Programmes are attended by over 100 colleagues a year. Research has shown that 70% of colleagues attending the PDP feel more engaged with the organisation and 15% have been promoted since attending.

Access membership has grown from about 250 in 2010 to over 1500 in 2014.

In 2011 LBG scored 92% in the Disability Standard (Business Disability Forum), was ranked joint 2nd (up from 74th in 2009), awarded best employer and private sector champion.

What do employees say?

"There is a blurred line between colleagues with disabilities and those without. We think it is nonsense to focus on the definition of someone's disability or health condition. We simply make the workplace more accessible, flexible and productive. This benefits everybody. We give colleagues with disabilities the tools to do the job, the training to get on and a support framework should they need it."
—John Turner, Chair, Access Network

What does Lloyds say?
"It makes business sense to help our colleagues with disabilities work effectively and contribute to the success of their teams and the Group. The measures we have put in place are helping us meet this goal and whilst there is still room for improvement we are pleased with the achievements we have made to date."—Mark Fisher, Director of Group Operations and Executive Sponsor for Disability

» *"The measures we have put in place are helping us meet this goal and whilst there is still room for improvement we are pleased with the achievements we have made to date"*

Accenture – Disability. It Happens campaign

Disability. It Happens. This was one of many campaigns the Accenture UKI Inclusion & Diversity Team ran in conjunction with the Accent on Enablement volunteer network. Over the course of one night, they put posters on each desk divider across its UKI campus (about 10,000 employees); they remained there for 12 months. Additionally, the pdf was shared across the global networks for updating with geographically relevant data, which increased the campaign's exposure to up to 281k staff globally.

The issue
Accenture has strong core values. One of these is 'Respect for the Individual'. The ambition of the Inclusion & Diversity programme is to ensure employees can turn up to work each day and focus on the job

at hand without having to negotiate obstacles that distract and at times might cause distress.

The idea
Accenture has an active Inclusion & Diversity team, which, in conjunction with the Accent on Enablement network (a volunteer network that supports people with visible and non-visible disabilities), ran a flagship event for International Day of Persons with Disabilities in December 2013. This event proved to be such a success that the Inclusion & Diversity team identified within Accenture an appetite for more knowledge sharing across the general population and a need to signpost line managers as well as disabled employees to the appropriate resources.

The driver
The Inclusion & Diversity team initiated and drove this campaign. Accenture are very keen to normalise visible and non-visible disabilities and eradicate the stigma associated with them. They recognise that each individual is unique, and that the role of the company is to support and recognise this as a source of innovation and creativity and to create an environment that allows all its employees to thrive.

Accenture has established disability networks in many countries. The UKI business is seen as leading the way in enablement, and they pilot many initiatives that are subsequently shared across the organisation. They work closely with HR, Employee Relations, Legal and Marketing to help navigate the new territory of the campaigns and to keep them on the right track. As they work toward their collective goal, they focus on ensuring that projects are treated as a cross team effort, which they consider critical to the delivery of robust and long term change.

The resources
The key resource requirement was for one employee to design and obtain global/local approvals for the production of the poster.

The deliverables
The deliverable was a simple pdf that could be shared across the globe and printed, laminated and displayed in offices.

What do employees say?
The benefits to employees were seen as significant for such a small campaign.

The campaign:
- reinforced the leadership's support of employees with disability
- increased awareness and understanding for all employees through access to the materials
- provided line managers with resource packs
- recognised the value of disabled employees and promoted membership to Access on Enablement

What does Accenture say?

"Accenture recognises that people thrive when they can bring their whole selves to work and we strive to make this a reality each and every day. Our people are our greatest asset and we treat them as such. We are committed to making Accenture an inclusive and supportive workplace where every employee is given an opportunity to grow and develop without barriers."—David Sawyer, Managing Director, Geographic Operations, UKI, Accenture Accent on Enablement Executive Sponsor

[SECTION SIX]

A FRESH RESPONSE

"First get your facts; then you can distort them at your leisure"—*Mark Twain*

Fresher statistics

So, you have read through the whole report and you still want to know how many disabled people you employ?

Let us try to help.

Four key things to keep in mind:
- While many employers will rely on numbers to build the business case for change, our research suggests that it is unlikely that employers will ever get accurate data;
- Disability and ill health is a fact of life – when and how individuals share personal information is part determined by how far they have assimilated that information themselves, how they feel about it and their perception about how others will react;
- Legislation requires employers to put adjustments in place – that is a fact: finding ways of making the process easy might result in better data over time, whether people need adjustments or not;
- The more that employers can work around the need for 'proof', the more likely they will focus on the key drivers of change.

The basics

If you work in an organisation that needs statistics to drive change, here are five of the best:
- 83 per cent of disabled people acquire their disability during their working lives;[15]
- 6.9 million disabled people in the UK are of working age;[16]
- 3.2 million disabled people of working age in the UK have a job;[17]
- In any workplace, between 11–12.9% of all employees are disabled employees;[18]
- One quarter of the 28 million workers in the UK, have a long term health condition or impairment.[19]

Key messages from the research
- Employers are unlikely to get a wholly accurate understanding about the number of disabled people in the workplace;

- Not having accurate numbers should not be used as an excuse for inaction. How an organisation delivers workplace adjustments should be constantly under review and any improvements made. Our learning suggest that a better system for delivering adjustments will also deliver better data;
- In the absence of accurate data, work on the premise that your workforce will be comprised of between 11–12.9% of disabled employees regardless of whether they know who they are or not and regardless of whether they choose to tell you or not;
- If you want to count and monitor things, shift the emphasis to the workplace adjustment process;
- If 'building a picture' about the prevalence of disability is still a helpful driver for change, try using the employee profiles developed by Business Disability Forum.[20] These are a useful 'map' and a good communications tool when talking to senior people about numbers.

Expert opinion

"Knowing someone has a visual impairment, arthritis or a mental health condition tells you very little about what they might need at work. However if you know what the barrier is, you are more likely to be able to determine the solution."
—**Susan Scott Parker, Business Disability Forum**

Fresher monitoring

"Science by itself is about numbers, and it's about measuring things. It's very important but it's very dry."—James Balog

Four key things to keep in mind:
- You need to be clear about purpose when formally monitoring – getting the purpose of the question right is the key for everything that follows;
- There is a difference between sharing information as part of an anonymous monitoring process and sharing information about your disability with your manager or asking for an adjustment – anonymous monitoring is important to get right but it isn't what keeps disabled people awake at night;
- Getting the tone and 'feel' of the question right is an important component in getting good data;
- Collecting data is often seen by employers as a transactional exercise – for employees it is an emotional transaction.

» **You need to be clear about purpose when formally monitoring**

> **Employer respondents**
>
> "Not many employees wish to share that they have a disability and this is reflected in the annual employee survey. It could be down to fear that they will be identified or that their career may suffer – we want to know what to do about that."
>
> "Our 'disclosure' rates are low and need to be improved – and we have inconsistent recording of those who have workplace adjustments."
>
> "We struggle to understand why people are hesitant to 'disclose'. Is it reasonable to assume that it is something to do with our culture rather than there just not being a mechanism through which they can officially 'declare'."

Our research showed that 73% of employer respondents have a system in place to monitor the number of disabled employees they have but 34% do not know how many disabled employee they have.

Over half (57%) of individual respondents said that the main reason why they shared information about their disability was that they needed their employer to make an adjustment for them.

Most disabled respondents (60%) who haven't shared information with their employer said that the main reason why they did not do so is that they would be worried that if they told their employer there may be repercussions either now, or in the future. Just 15% say it is because they do not see it as relevant to tell their employer.

» **Fear may be exacerbated by a lack of clarity around the purpose of the questions being asked as well as insufficient explanation about what will be done with the data**

Fear may be exacerbated by a lack of clarity around the purpose of the questions being asked as well as insufficient explanation about what will be done with the data. Nearly half (42%) of respondents reported not knowing why they are being asked. Nearly two-thirds (63%) said that either some people will always resist the label 'disabled' or think the association with the word is a big personal step.

It is therefore critical to be clear on the purpose of questions in both formal monitoring exercises or in other areas.

Why do employers monitor?

Employers use data in all types of ways. But as we have seen it is important that the data is accurate. Inaccurate data is misleading and even dangerous. It may result in one or all of the following:

- A cultural belief that very few disabled people, or people with a health condition work for the organisation;
- Inaccurate assumptions that disabled people don't want to or can't work well in certain trades or sectors;
- Disproportionate efforts to recruit disabled people externally – "we better 'fix this'" by recruiting disabled people because we don't have any";

- Apparent low numbers of disabled people in an organisation implying there is no need for a high quality adjustment processes when the opposite might be true;
- No plan to target appropriate pay, progression and reward strategies for disabled employees;
- Lack of plans that focus on the retention and career development of disabled employees with no specific learning and development initiatives provided in the same way as for women or black and minority ethnic employees;
- Fear that low numbers or lack of data will become public and cause reputational damage.

Anonymous sharing

Employers may choose to conduct formal monitoring exercises as part of a requirement or commitment to 'monitor' protected characteristic data and publish trends. This is usually done by anonymous surveys and is not about individual needs.

Evidence shows that when surveys are anonymous employers are likely to get better data than from surveys which are not anonymous.

Participation will also be affected by the explanation of the purpose of the survey, the ease of the process, clarity about how the information will be used and who will have it and assurances that there are no repercussion to sharing information.

Formal recording systems

Employers are increasingly using HR self-recording systems that allow employees to upload their diversity characteristics.

Our research suggests that the data is of a variable quality and usefulness because the methods for securing the data are rarely systematic and they are not seen as anonymous. The quality of the descriptions about what constitutes disability is also varied and often inadequate.

As with anonymous sharing, participation in formal recording systems is affected by the explanation of the purpose, clarity about how the information will be used and who will have it and assurances that there are no adverse repercussions to sharing information. Good participation also requires repeated and meaningful communications about the importance of uploading personal data.

In order to be useful, formal recording systems also require quality signposting to where individuals may source support or access to a workplace adjustment process. Indeed, if an employee indicates they are disabled on a non-anonymous system then the employer should contact them to ensure they have any adjustments that they may require.

Individual sharing with colleagues and line managers

Quite apart from the sharing of information for formal monitoring purposes, employees and their managers will also need confidence in other processes that may exist for sharing personal information (or when a disability becomes apparent), especially in relation to how workplace adjustments are sought and secured.

Build a virtuous circle of trust

Our research indicated that a high proportion of disabled employees will assume that the sharing of their personal information at an individual level will be 'recorded' and acted upon somewhere so employers need to ensure that messages are clear.

Building trust

The key to building better data is to ensure systematic and consistent processes.

In anonymous surveys and self-service systems employers must be clear why they ask for information and what will be done with it, by whom, and by when. To build a virtuous circle of trust, the organisation should routinely share progress made and actions taken as a consequence of monitoring.

In addition, employers must have an easy route to support people to share information about their disability at any point in their employment whether they have shared that information previously, or not. Easy to use, clear, transparent processes to secure adjustments are also essential in building a trust cycle.

Take account of the enduring human resisters

Our research suggests that some employees will always choose not to share information when they can avoid doing so.

Some do not want to associate with the term 'disability'. Others might fit the 'disability definition' and associate with it but not need adjustments. Others will have highly developed personal strategies in place in managing others and challenging situations. The fact is they have a right not to share.

How to ask the questions

If you are conducting a formal monitoring process about the number of disabled employees you have, then you will get more accurate results if you make it clear that disability is broad and covers lots of common conditions. A simple yes/no disability question won't get you very far at all but there's no simple short-hand and you will need to find your own ways of asking.

We came across some imaginative communications from the employer partners. One example of the kind of question you might use is:

> *"Do you have a disability, long-term injury or health condition? This could be a physical or mental condition and includes common conditions like dyslexia, cancer, depression, diabetes, back problems, heart problems to name just a few examples."*

Some employers also use the phrase "or consider yourself to be disabled". This adds further potential for less accurate results if, for example, someone reads it and thinks 'well I'm deaf but no, I don't consider myself to be disabled'.

Expert opinion

Statistics don't tell us the whole story. For example, everyone knows someone who has or has had cancer and yet how would you answer the question 'How common is cancer?' We might say "'More than 1 in 3 people in the UK will develop some form of cancer during their lifetime". It makes the point with regard to prevalence but it doesn't tell you much about what has to be done, and by whom, in the context of work.

Employers might accept that disability is everywhere and that it affects everyone but they might want to make sure that they are recruiting disabled people and retaining them when they acquire a disability. The key is to do this in a meaningful way.

At Business Disability Forum we have always made it clear that there is no "magic" wording that you can use to ensure you get wholly accurate figures about the number of disabled people that you may be employing. For example when collecting evidence from members with regard to the Disability Standard we deliberately choose not to ask about the number of disabled people organisations employ. The number doesn't tell you much in isolation. What we focus on is whether organisations know how long it takes to agree (or not agree) and implement adjustments. Of those employers who undertake the Disability Standard only 37% know how long it takes to agree and implement adjustments.

For us, it is not about whether to monitor or not, it's about starting somewhere entirely different.
—**Brendan Roach, Senior Disability Consultant, Business Disability Forum**

Employee respondent

"I want my employer to be crystal clear each time they ask, why they are asking – if it is to monitor, identify and interpret trends, then be clear that this is the purpose, state how the information will be used and report back progress.

If it is part of a process to ensure employees can secure the workplace adjustments they need, then again be clear this is the purpose of asking, signpost to the process and include it when you ask people about their disability and your commitment to confidentiality about what is shared."

Expert opinion

"Employers need to understand that people are quite rightly wary about divulging personal information without know who is going to see it and how it is going to be used. In many ways the old saying that "information is power" is true. An employee who tells their employer that they have a disability or health condition may feel they will be vulnerable and at risk of discrimination – and they might be right. Good people working for employers may find this shocking but for many disabled people this is reality.

Before starting on a monitoring exercise ask yourself why you want to know how many disabled people (or indeed any other type of person) works for your organisation. What does that information tell you about your organisation and what are you going to do with it? If you want to make your organisation more diverse and one that welcomes and values difference you have to walk the walk first. Show your employees that that this is a great place to work for everyone and that you will be flexible and accommodating and then ask them to tell you about their disability – you'll get a better response. You might find, however, that you no longer feel the need to ask people who work for you about their disability/religious beliefs/sexuality anymore."
— **Bela Gor, Legal Director, Business Disability Forum**

Key messages from the research

- Most employers have some system in place to monitor or track the number of disabled people they have and are saying that if they don't, they won't know what is going on and what needs to be improved.
- For employers this is often planned as a "data collection exercise" but for employees it is often an emotional transaction and will often result in personal reflection and occasionally people seeking advice.
- Disability, injury, accident and ill health is a fact of life, it can happen to anyone at any time and often does, so any monitoring system needs to start with messages that communicate that fact and which emphasise that disability at work is very, very 'normal'.
- In order to build trust and confidence, employers should provide explicit assurances that sharing information about disability will not have adverse consequences, particularly in economically difficult periods.
- Employers should explicitly explain to staff that their sharing information about disability, even if they require no adjustments at the present time, is still a helpful indicator to the employer as they develop ongoing recruitment and engagement strategies.
- Employers should try to think more creatively about the use of the word 'disability' in their communications.

- Employers should routinely report back both to the workforce and individuals on the plans and progress following the analysis of information from monitoring exercises and specifically describe how the information has added value.
- If employers cannot routinely report back in this way, they should revisit the purposes for which the data is collected and/or the reason for asking for information.
- When individuals share information about their disability the statistic that results is really just the number of people who believe they are disabled by whatever criteria you've chosen to use and who are content to tell you about it. This doesn't mean it's not worth asking but it does need to be understood for what it is. It could be benchmarked year on year. It reflect employees' level of understanding about what disability is and/or their trust in how their employer will respond to such information. What it isn't necessarily is a reflection of the number *of people* who are disabled within your workforce.

A fresher workplace adjustment process

> *"Next to doing the right thing, the most important thing is let people know you are doing the right thing."*—John D Rockefeller

You are now on the home straight and you want to improve the visibility and integrity of the workplace adjustment process. Four things to keep in mind:
- Our research shows that the main reason that employees tell their employer about their disability is because they need an adjustment. That means its important to get the delivery process right;
- Our research suggests that employees want their employer to 'normalise' the process for seeking and securing workplace adjustments;
- In addition to wanting the process 'normalised', employees would like their employers to focus on the quality and consistency of delivery – in terms of visibility, ease of access, timescales and levels of effectiveness;
- The 'name' of the process (of ensuring employees can access adjustments that are reasonable) might contribute to the 'mood music' for how employees will trust the level of fairness of the eventual outcome (and whether to use it at all).

Our research showed that 22 out of 55 employers monitor the number of adjustments requested and 23 out of 55 employers monitor the number of adjustments provided. However only 18% monitor data about the speed and quality of adjustments made.

With 57% of respondents saying that the main reason why they share information about their disability is that they need their employer to make an adjustment for them it is vital that employers would do better to monitor the workplace adjustment process. Respondents were keen to stress that they want the employer to 'normalise' the requests for adjustments. As one respondent said, "Why should it be any different from requesting any other piece of equipment to do your job?."

> **The key is to ensure that the decision making process is fair, consistent, effective, transparent and timely**

Tackling inconsistent processes

One of the common themes that came up from the survey was that employers wanted to improve the consistency of the delivery of their workplace adjustment process. Several mentioned that they had just started or were due to start root and branch reviews. Several had a newly identified 'process' owner.

While recommendations regarding the positioning of the process are beyond the scope of this study, we did observe that a number of 'shifts' are happening in terms of the location of the workplace adjustment process, or improvements to ownership.

Several employers have started to centralise processes that had previously been localised. The most frequently cited reason was to remove the responsibility of deciding what is reasonable or not from busy line managers and thus increase the speed of delivery. Employers also recognised that centralised processes provide a greater opportunity to purchase more cost-effectively and monitor costs more consistently, particularly the costs of assessments which are not very often required.

The key is to ensure that the decision making process is fair, consistent, effective, transparent and timely.

One employer mentioned how one employee had awaited 18 months to see whether they could be provided with a computer mouse costing £300. They had been off work throughout that period. A peer review exercise to determine the lessons learnt suggested the following:

- The manager had been worried that the purchasing of a mouse would lead to further requests from other employees;
- The IT department had disputed the quality and effectiveness of the product requested;
- Nobody had 'ownership' in maintaining dialogue with the employee regarding the adjustment process and outcome.

The lessons from this are obvious.

What should the process be called?

There is strong evidence from the survey that employees make sense of how accommodating their employer is, or is likely to be, by looking for clues in how easy, or difficult it is to 'be someone who is different.'

The majority of people with a disability or health condition will acquire or develop it while in work. This process will require a period of reflection and readjustment to things that had previously been taken for granted. This can take time – months or even years.

Our recommendation would be to make it as easy as possible to offer employees access to things that will allow them the opportunity to retain and maintain their work. One way of doing this is to 'normalise' and make more attractive the process that is available to secure workplace adjustments.

Our recommendation would be to call the process the 'workplace adjustment process'.

This does not erode the current principle that employers are the final decision-makers as to whether an adjustment is reasonable. However, shifting the emphasis might make it easier for people to access the process and remove anxiety from the vast majority of employees for whom an adjustment can be made at no, or low, cost.

> **Expert opinion**
>
> "As a lawyer I am so used to the term 'reasonable adjustments' that I ignore its connotations for disabled employees. As a disabled person, I can recognise the temptation of minimising my requests rather than have them rejected as 'unreasonable'. Employers send a great message if they simply offer disabled staff 'workplace adjustments." —**Caroline Gooding, Lawyer**

What is the average cost of workplace adjustments?
Less than you think, probably.

We have not come across a significant amount of public, well-tested and consistent information regarding the average cost of a workplace adjustment for disabled employees. Of the material we did find, there is very little description of how the 'average cost' was reached. Certainly we do not believe there is a universal understanding of what constituents an 'average cost' within the employers' community.

Some employers might, for example, use the concept of 'average cost' but exclude the costs of managing the process. Others might exclude the cost of assessment. Others might include the cost of assessment even when the outcome then suggests that an assessment may not have been needed.

You may wonder how valuable data on 'average' cost is anyway. Average salary or average customer spend are not, alone, particularly useful figures either.

However, for those employers who do wish to develop a better understanding of the average costs of workplace adjustments it is important to remember:

- To factor in all the employees for whom even those whose adjustments cost nothing. All the evidence suggests that this is the most frequent type of adjustment. An example of this could be flexible start and finish times to avoid peak travel or changing the location of someone's desk;
- That the cost of assessing someone may be a one-off cost but needs to be seen in the context of the value it brings over the entire course of their continued employment;
- The cost of not making the adjustment – which may result in additional time to complete work, lost productivity, reduced collaborative team working and in a frustrated, de-motivated employee who does not feel empowered to request the adjustment. It may even result in a retention and/or legal risk;
- The opportunity cost of someone off work and unproductive whilst waiting for a decision on an adjustment.

When looking at average costs we would encourage employers to compare costs with the ongoing value of retention and sustained employment of talented disabled people and those with a health condition.

It is the value of retention that would determine a more accurate picture of the adjustment costs employers are making.

What should a workplace adjustment process include?

The detail of creating an end-to-end workplace adjustment process is beyond the scope of this project. The work being done by Business Disability Forum in association with it's members and partners is encouraging.

But it must be in the DNA of the organisation – enabling people to 'be themselves' at work in the knowledge that they can request adjustments to how they work. This checklist offers our view of the key things to get right and often cited by the survey respondents:

- A widely known and accessible adjustment process available to all employees in the same way as anything else is (and not hidden away under the disability section of the website). Occasional reminders about where it can be found in general communications;
- A process owner and adequate resourcing – preferably a central funding system;
- Information about the 'soft' and 'hard' types of adjustments that managers are authorised to action quickly without referral upwards;
- An understanding of how to differentiate between a 'want' and a 'need' and a process for denying unreasonable requests;
- A way of differentiating between those adjustments that might be fast-tracked as well as those that might require assessment
- Strong review and feedback mechanisms;
- A way of capturing agreements made and a way to make it easy for employees to 'induct' or 'educate' their incoming line managers;
- A bank of case studies about the most common adjustments that can be made particularly helpful for those with a new disability or new to adjustments and looking for advice about what can be put in place to help them flourish at work.

[SECTION SEVEN]

FEELING DISABILITY-CONFIDENT NOW?

"You can't start the next chapter of your life if you keep re-reading the last one"—*Anon*

From 'getting in' to 'getting on'

Kate Nash Associates gets to hear what the key topics of debate are for disabled employees. One that dominates is the workplace adjustment process.

While this debate is critical, and one for employees and networks to contribute to, it keeps talent 'stuck' in the 'domestic' debate. Moreover it skews the nature of debate between people of different protected characteristics. Proportionality of talent is a common theme across the diversity and inclusion spectrum but you rarely find other groups discussing the fundamental topic of getting into a building or accessing the company website. We need to get a wiggle on now and shift the debate from 'getting in' to 'getting on'.

Disability-confident employers

Business Disability Forum[21] first started to use the concept of 'disability confidence' some years ago. It was conceived of by Susan Scott-Parker the chief executive. For them it is a concept that supports an employer to:
- Understand that disability impacts all parts of the business;
- Identify, and remove barriers, for groups of people;
- Be willing and able to make adjustments for individuals;
- Not make assumptions based on peoples' disability.

The use of the term, together with Business Disability Forum's enabling products, and their unique approach to systems thinking have helped hundreds of employers to deploy a systematic approach to removing the barriers to both individuals and groups of disabled employees at work.

In July 2013 the government launched a two-year Disability Confident campaign. The germ of the idea for the campaign came from Business

> » We need to get a wiggle on now and shift the debate from 'getting in' to 'getting on'

These things can be complex but it's hardly rocket science

Disability Forum's President's Group dinner hosted by Fujitsu in January 2013 which the then Secretary of State and Minister of Disabled People attended.

While some of the original four key principles have got a little lost in the national roll-out of the campaign it has nonetheless been a very positive contribution to the process of engaging with UK employers who want to champion the skills of disabled people.

Now is the time to mine this concept to everyone's advantage. Now is the time to frame some new conversations about how to 'get on', rather than 'get in'. Now is the time to create a common understanding about the characteristics of both organisational and individual confidence at work rather than get stuck on basic housekeeping matters.

Individuals and those running networks and resource groups will always have a role in supporting an organisation to improve its workplace adjustment process and the quality of policy and delivery. But if disabled employees get stuck in the merry-go-round debate about the adjustment process it's almost the same as colluding with the view that it's too difficult to get right?

Six years ago Kate Nash Associates conducted a review for an organisation about the key barriers disabled employees were facing at work. A real bugbear was a restrictive travel and expenses policy that took no account of the extra costs of travelling for some disabled employees. We created a plan of action. Last year we went back to review progress with the same organisation.

Guess what was the bugbear was?

Of course these things can be complex but it's hardly rocket science.

Disability-confident employees

We asked some of the survey participants and network leaders what would happen if employers and employees together chose to improve the balance of the debate and to move it from 'getting in' to 'getting on'. These were some of their reactions:

"The adjustment process is a dominant conversation – it would be helpful to leave that conversation for the business to get right and instead do some of the developmental work with our members in the same way as other resource groups do – talent management, leadership development, personal effectiveness."

"My employer is amazing but you can only change yourself at the end of the day – it's about how you deal with life and how you chose to play the hand of cards that you are dealt with – that isn't popular to say when there is a whole industry our there set up and funded to get disabled people into work but if we can, we need to remove ourselves from being the subjects of 'how to be helped' to the drivers of helping ourselves. This was the fundamental principle behind the fight for anti-discrimination legislation. It's taken another 20 years for us to work out it continues to be a fundamental principle behind human growth and learning at work."

We also asked them their views about what makes a disability confident employee. We summarise their contributions in appendix five and offer a model of understanding about what constitutes a disability confident disabled person.

It can take a lot of confidence for disabled people to be themselves at work and to take the step to ask for support or adjustments. It takes courage to do the things we have to do as humans to remind other humans that we are all human beings in the game of life.

Stories and moments in history often help us make sense of our capacity to anticipate, accommodate and celebrate human difference and we don't have to look far for inspiration.

Over half a century ago, on 1st December 1955 Rosa Parks refused to obey a bus driver's order to give up her seat in the 'colored' section to a white passenger. She was subsequently arrested and her defiance became a symbol of the modern civil rights movement. Eight years later Martin Luther King delivered his 'I have a dream speech'. And fifty years later the USA swore in its first black president. Still, there is a long way to go.

Rosa's individual act of 'being herself' by sitting where she wanted, and the many other individual acts of others who took risks triggered a sea-change that helped millions that came after – it got easier.

This story has much to offer millions of disabled employees who feel unable to share information about their disability, nervous about what the repercussions might be.

It is individuals who drive change for themselves and for others. And it starts with confidence, sometimes courage.

Over the last two years or so there has been a steady trickle of senior executives who have begun to talk openly about their experiences of ill-health, depression and disability. We mentioned Andrew McDonald in section three. In addition, John Binns, a former equity partner at Deloitte UK, has become a formidable ambassador in the mental health debate, the Time to Change campaign and the establishment of the City Mental Health Alliance. Iain Wilkie, senior partner at EY stimulated the creation of the Employers Stammering Network. Brian Heyworth, Global Co-head of Financial Institutions Group, Global Banking, HSBC speaks openly about his positive experiences of mental health and is breaking new ground in making it easier for others to share experiences.

The Be Yourself campaign created by Shell, stimulated by the Secrets & Big News project is a great example of the force for change that comes when people can be themselves at work. It takes individuals to create change.

Networks – what's in a name?

Disabled employee networks[22] are growing steadily in the UK. We work with 300 across the public and private sector. One of the things we have noticed is that many networks or resource groups struggle with decisions about the name which of course reflects the 'brand' of the network.

We suggested in section four (idea 15) that when people buy products we are drawn to a brand and the art of brand creation is about tapping into deep human desires and aspirations. Branding is about drawing people to something unique, special, 'stand-out' and seductive. Professional brand creators know that humans buy things for all kinds of reasons which are often tied up with how we are perceived, as much as the usefulness of the product.

We come across many networks who strive too hard to remove or play with the word "disability" in the name of the network. We see many permutations and combinations of the word – using lower case and uppercase letters. They are all struggling to convey talent and ability. But maybe we are missing a trick?

Our research suggests that as humans we simply don't gravitate to the word disability and even when individuals are technically covered by the definition in the Equality Act, because it takes people a long time to understand that what you are experiencing is the same as the legal definition it can take years to associate with the word. Moreover our research suggests that some people will never associate with the language.

So why use it to brand networks? Might it have direct impact on the outcomes and success of the network? Is it time to think differently about the language used to brand networks?

The expression "the lady doth protest too much, methinks" is a quotation from the 1602 play "Hamlet" by William Shakespeare. It has subsequently been used as a figure of speech to indicate that a person's overly frequent or vehement attempts to convince others of something have ironically helped to convince others that the opposite is true, by making the person look insincere or defensive.

If networks put ABILITY in capital letters and the prefix "dis" in lower case might that be perceived the same way?

Why not use the phrase purple networks? If it makes it easier for people to get involved, get what they need, support the business in its journey of disability confidence why not? If the phrase 'purple talent' like the phrase 'purple pound' helps employers to do what they need to do to cross the line, why not? It does nothing to erode the basic premise of what disability means in the Equality Act. That is not what this is about.

The Channel 4 series "The Last Leg" is a good example of making it easier for us all to talk about this stuff, and to give people permission to ask relevant and human questions. If the same series was called "Laughing at Disabled People" I doubt whether many would tune in – it wasn't. Their brand experts got their first and it has been a hit.

The third phase of change – thanks for the warm up

Talking of Channel 4, do you remember their trailer for the Paralympics following the Olympics? It teased us with the line "Thanks for the warm up". It was naughty. It was exciting. It told the story about how far disabled people have come in claiming their own place in the world. It conveyed competition, power and the thrill of a new dawn.

I think we are entering a third phase in building sustainable culture change in recruiting and developing disabled employees.

The first phase was the establishment of equalities legislation secured in 1995 and now harmonised under the Equality Act 2010.

The second phase has been the process by which employers have become, and continue to become, disability confident organisations through the systematic use of best practice tools and enabling products. That phase continues.

Meanwhile, the third phase has begun. It is the phase when disabled employees shape their powerful stories and describe their truth and their world so that organisations just "get it" and want to invest in their talent, their career, their progression.

In other words, "Thanks for the warm up…"

Many of the networks we come across want to leave the narrative about workplace adjustments to the "process engineers" within an organisation. Sometimes those folk are based in human resource departments, sometimes diversity and inclusion, sometimes in occupational health, and sometimes in a different place entirely. Disabled people want to spend more time to talk about strategies for career progression:

- practical ways to bypass the 'human resisters' that exist – how to just move round the mountain when colleagues are uncomfortable with difference;
- how to create new toolkits to help share learning and tips about how to transcend other peoples pity or discomfort;
- passing on learning to those who may be newly diagnosed with a health condition to ask for and secure adjustments that help people to get on;
- how to give assurances that adjustments will result in your continued productivity even when you are unsure yourself;
- talking to others about what it means to be disability confident.

And in this third phase, we must not forget the vital role that non-disabled colleagues play in supporting the story of change. For some people that can often be of more help than the views and counsel of disabled people. Some of the mentoring schemes we came across provide disabled and non-disabled mentors for that reason.

The concept of 'straight allies' developed by Stonewall[23] has been an enormously helpful one. 'Straight ally' is a term used to describe heterosexual people who believe that lesbian, gay and bisexual people should experience full equality in the workplace. In their view "good straight allies" recognise that gay people can perform better if they can be themselves and straight allies use their role within an organisation to create a culture where this can happen. Straight allies might be at the very top of an organisation or a colleague in a team. Either way, they recognise that it's not just the responsibility of gay people to create a workplace culture that is inclusive of everyone.

We need purple allies too.

As I finish, it is worth pointing out that I have managed to get to the end of this publication with hardly a mention of the social model of disability and yet the model runs through me like Brighton through a stick of rock.

Its strengths and weaknesses are well documented. The concept will forever be the lynchpin in the campaign towards anti-discrimination legislation.

I believe the next major advances for disabled people both in and out of work will come from three things. It will come from employers embracing the specific four principles that make up the concept of disability

» **We need purple allies too**

confidence. It will come from the roll-out of imaginative campaigns to highlight the concept and the underpinning principles, supported by successive governments over time. And it will come from the conversations between disabled employees themselves and greater engagement between employer and employee.

It won't be welfare reform that will create the major advancements. It won't be training line managers to become disability confident. It won't be a reform of the government's Two Tick scheme. It won't be a fresh Work Programme.

These things will help but it will be the conversations between disabled employees across organisations and businesses in the UK and globally that will drive the pace and texture for the third phase of change.

Throughout my career I have had the very great honour of working with hundreds of non-disabled allies. Their grit and determination to build disability confident workplaces is breathtaking. In suggesting that the third phase requires more conversation across the community of purple talent, it also requires deeper conversations with our purple allies. Together we just might create a wildfire.

Postscript

In section one "Gilly's story" was used as a way of illustrating reactions that many individuals will receive when sharing information at work. The name of the person has been changed. This was the reply written by Kate Nash to help an old mentor, and friend to help her daughter to manage a process that is all too common.

Having read this book, what would you write?

Email reply to Gilly's Mum

From: Kate Nash [mailto:Kate@KateNashAssociates.com]
Sent: Monday, August 06, 2012 10:32 AM
To:
Subject: RE: Hello!

If I were her, I would do two things:

Firstly I would send a really positive and thankful memo to the head of HR thanking her for sending a note about her (impairment). In this note she must suggest that she has been reflecting on the impact that the note may have had on others and has been wondering if they could together have had a better outcome if she had been involved in preparing such a note. She may want to offer the fact that, of course (impairment) affects different people in different ways and she is skilled and confident in managing her condition and needs very few [or any???] workplace adjustments.

She can then nip in the bud any accusation of not sharing this information at interview by demonstrating her knowledge that she did not need to. She might want to end the note by again thanking the head of HR and asking if she can be involved in any further dissemination of personal information in order to help reduce unnecessary and unhelpful impact on others (or something like that). She must copy in her boss but not refer to her bosses suggestion that she should share this information with HR.

Secondly I would send a brief note to her boss saying that she was surprised to have been quizzed by someone doing a risk assessment who seems to suggest that she should now share personal information even more widely? She is wondering if there is some kind of problem? What would be the purpose behind sharing her personal information with the top team? This is not usual practice elsewhere… given that she does not need any workplace adjustments is there a lack of experience about managing disabled people at work and the duties of (organisation). She would be more than happy to help people understand the stability of her condition and how it impacts on her at work so that people understand it isn't a problem that people seem to be suggesting it might be… that she is confused by these actions so far… would her boss be happy to mentor her in order to ensure she tells the people that need to know while providing the dignity she needs to do her job well.

Incidentally, tell her from me she is not weak – she has (impairment) – and finding away through this stuff will be a feature of her working life. Developing active strategies for dealing with others will help build her esteem and protect her from too much of an ongoing conversation about all this. If she practices and gets this right she will learn well for the future. Active management of her controlling her own story is the key – it won't go away so best find personal strategies for dealing with other peoples soft bigotry of low expectations.

I stress this would be my personal strategy – but I have been around the block and it wouldn't suit everyone.

> *"Tact is the ability to tell someone to go to hell in such a way that they look forward to the trip"*—Winston Churchill

Endnotes

1. *Why Are You Pretending To Be Normal?*, Phil Friend OBE and Dave Rees
2. *Disability in the United Kingdom*, Papworth, 2010
3. Labour Force Survey, Quarter 2, 2012
4. The disability and health employment strategy, Department for Work and Pensions, 2013
5. Labour Force Survey, Quarter 2, 2012
6. The nine protected characteristics are: age, disability, gender reassignment, marriage and civil partnership, pregnancy and maternity, race, religion and belief, sex, sexual orientation.
7. Labour Force Survey, Quarter 2, 2012
8. www.goodpeople.co.uk
9. www.itgetsbetter.org
10. www.stonewall.org.uk/at_home/3460.asp
11. www.bbc.co.uk/news/blogs-ouch-25812302
12. www.youtube.com/watch?v=qbC4irVmsXU
13. http://businessdisabilityforum.org.uk/employee-engagement/employers-disability-the-law
14. http://resources.civilservice.gov.uk/wp-content/uploads/2011/07/130906Recording-Personal-Data-Information-Pack-FINAL1.doc
15. http://resources.civilservice.gov.uk/wp-content/uploads/2011/07/130906RP-DLEAFLETFINAL.pdf
16. *Disability in the United Kingdom*, Papworth, 2010
17. https://www.gov.uk/government/news/more-than-500-disabled-people-a-week-supported-into-work-or-training
18. The disability and health employment strategy, Department for Work and Pensions, 2013
19. Labour Force Survey, Quarter 2, 2012
20. The disability and health employment strategy, Department for Work and Pensions, 2013
21. www.businessdisabilityforum.co.uk
22. www.businessdisabilityforum.org.uk
23. Sometimes called business resource groups or affinity groups, or special interest groups
24. www.stonewall.co.uk

Appendix one

Secrets & Big News Advisory Board

They say many hands make light work and so it was with the Secrets & Big News Advisory Board who steered the project from start to finish over two years. Kate Nash Associates is grateful to each and every member of the SBN Advisory Board.

- Sally Ward, BT
- Brendan Roach, Business Disability Forum
- Robert Tate, Business in the Community
- Paul Willgoss, Civil Service Disability Network
- Matthew Thomas, Coca-Cola
- Angela Kefford-Watson, Kate Nash Associates
- John Turner, Lloyds Banking Group
- Andy Garrett, Metropolitan Police
- Andy Kneen, Shell
- Joanna Wootten, Solutions Included

Thanks also go to:

- Report and project sponsors: PwC LLP, Microlink, Metropolitan Police, BT, Post Office Ltd
- Charlotte Turner, Bean Research – who supported the research and analysis
- Kate Morgan, PhD research student, Leeds – who supported the research and analysis
- Susan Scott-Parker, CEO, Business Disability Forum – who supported the project with key staff and expert counsel
- Janet Hill, Department for Work and Pensions and Lin Homer, HMRC – who invited government departments to take part
- Shell, EDF Energy, Coca-Cola, PwC, and Fujitsu who helped host focus groups and to all the participants
- Jim Pollard, Not Only Word who edited the publication
- Angela Whitney, Polly Jackson, Rachel Bray, Tom Hampson at Soapbox who designed and produced the publication

And for inspiration, thanks to:

Fiona Anderson, Sonia Bate, David Caldwell, Jane Campbell, Beth Carruthers, Helen Cherry, Helen Chipchase, Karen Coley, Joe Conner, Angela Cooke, Helen Cooke, Zoe Davies, Gary Denton, Mark Doughty, Caroline Dove, Paul Farmer, Caroline Gooding, Bela Gor, Vanessa Hardy, Jo Harry, Brian Heyworth, Giles Long, Janie Malherbe Jenson, Angela Matthews, Andrew McDonald, Toby Mildon, Simon Minty, Chris Moon, Fiona Morden, Mary-Anne Rankin, Jeanette Rosenberg, Liz Sayce, Paul Scantlebury, Nasser Siabi, Richard Tyrie, Graeme Whippy. And especially the 2,511 disabled employee survey respondents.

Appendix two

We are enormously grateful to the 55 employer partners who worked with us and shared information, thoughts, ideas and time to help shape and create the messages. The report is a summation of many conversations and discussions over a two-year period.

While their involvement does not constitute endorsement of the final report we hope they enjoy some of the big ideas and continue on their energetic journey of change and development.

- Accenture
- American Express
- Bank of England
- Barclays
- Barts Health NHS Trust
- BBC
- BT Group plc
- British Airways
- Big Lottery Fund
- Central London Community Healthcare NHS Trust
- Central and North West London NHS Foundation Trust
- Chelsea and Westminster Hospital NHS Foundation Trust
- Civil Aviation Authority
- CGI
- Crown Prosecution Service
- Deloitte LLP
- Department of Energy and Climate Change
- Defra
- Department for Business, Innovation and Skills
- Department for Education
- Department for Transport
- Department for Work and Pensions
- DVLA
- EDF Energy
- Environment Agency
- E.ON
- EY
- Eversheds LLP
- Fujitsu
- GSK
- Health and Safety Executive
- House of Commons
- Home Office
- HSBC Bank
- HMRC
- HM Treasury
- Islington Council
- Kings College Hospital NHS Foundation Trust
- KPMG LLP
- Leicestershire Police
- Lloyds Banking Group
- London Borough of Richmond upon Thames
- Metropolitan Police
- Ministry of Justice
- Motability Operations
- National Grid
- Post Office Limited
- The Royal Bank of Scotland Group
- Sainsburys Supermarkets Ltd
- Santander UK
- Scottish Government
- Shell
- Standard Chartered Bank
- Thomson Reuters
- Welsh Government

Appendix three

Approach to the study

In February 2013 Kate Nash Associates invited 100 employers to take part in the Secrets & Big News research project. The employer participants were drawn from KNA's extensive reach across its client and contact base.

There was no direct cost to take part in the project, other than a time commitment to complete a broad questionnaire about challenges and current practice with regard to monitoring, and time to circulate a second survey to disabled employees.

55 employers took part and together they reached a total of 2,511 disabled employees who responded to the survey. The Advisory Board had set a target of 500 responses so the reach far exceeded expectation.

The initial findings of the survey were shared with employer partners during six focus groups in October 2013. 41 employers took part in the focus groups with members of the advisory board, to discuss the early findings and hear their reactions and ideas to incorporate in the publication.

All information from respondents has been kept in complete confidence. The employer case studies mentioned in this report have been incorporated with the employers' permission. They are included to illustrate interesting and creative examples of what some organisations are doing; we found many more examples that could have been included.

Where we use quotes from the disabled employee respondents, we have kept them anonymous.

Secrets & Big News was not designed to be an academic study. The key purpose of the project is to stimulate a fresh debate on the issue often referred to a 'disclosure' and 'declaration' of disability in the workplace. One of the key hypotheses has been that the way we communicate and engage with our employees has a direct bearing on the process of securing information about who they are as well as how we can support people at work.

While the 55 employer partners that participated vary in terms of size, sector and type of trade Kate Nash Associates does not claim that the study is representative of employers in the UK as a whole. We encourage stakeholders to notice the themes and trends and build their own ideas and actions to build better monitoring processes and/or to enable people to be themselves for personal and business impact.

Appendix four

Executive summary of the top recommendations for employers

Don't make assumptions
1. Do not assume that low numbers of recorded disabled employees is an indicator that something is wrong with the recruitment process or there is a silver-bullet question that will yield 100% accuracy when monitoring – deciding whether to share information about disability, or not, is complex
2. Do not assume that low numbers is a comment on your trade, sector, size of organisation or the economy
3. Do not assume the words diversity and inclusion are helpful for people to understand that "this means people like me" – be specific when you engage with disabled employees

Think about the language
1. Don't use the words 'disclosure' or 'declaration' – it suggests that you think your employees have a secret or a big piece of news in relation to disability and ill health
2. Don't prefix the adjustment process with the words 'reasonable'
3. Don't get hung-up on the word disability

Notice the human resisters and make it easier for people to be themselves
1. Recognise that many individuals will need to build confidence and resilience in sharing their story of difference before sharing personal information more widely – and that they often find more skilful ways to do this over time
2. Stimulate and invest in employee networks and resource groups. Provide opportunities for employees to exchange ideas with others who have experience of managing their impairment at work and have successfully navigated their way through the "perception and adjustment maze" as well as what adjustments might help them

Be systematic and proactive
1. Find lots of ways to be specific and positive about disabled talent: show that you have a good understanding of the different experiences disabled employees have at work and do things that suggest that you 'get it' – profile their stories, provide case studies, keep it real
2. Ensure the availability of the workplace adjustment process is visible and accessible. Communicate the adjustments that are available without requiring people to rigidly define themselves as 'disabled'. Many individuals do not gravitate to or believe the word 'disability' refers to them
3. Communicate the fact that you expect 'difference' in the workplace – it is normal and to be celebrated. People who have a health condition

or disability are watching and learning how it is 'to be a disabled person round here' – and their judgment about an organisations level of disability confidence will have a direct impact on whether they tell their employer, or not – promote positive role models
4. Educate and develop line managers on the types of adjustments that can be provided in the workplace

If you monitor
1. If you monitor, be clear about the purpose and how information from employees will be used. Be clear that this is different from requests for adjustments or telling colleagues about your disability. Tell participants that monitoring might be used for better planning, understanding trends, removing barriers for groups of people
2. Tell employees that sharing information about disability will not have a negative outcome. Remember that many disabled employees do not share information because they think, by doing so, it will have a negative effect on their career, so tell them it won't
3. People assume (and want to assume) that if they have told one part of the organisation about their disability that this information will be passed on and be known by other parts of the organisation, but in reality few organisations are like this and employees often feel there are expected to justify their needs over and over again. Provide a point of contact and make available an in-house expert or confidential channel of information other than the line manager to help people think this through

Appendix five

Disability confident employees – a matrix of understanding

Earlier in the report we suggested that it may now be helpful for disability networks/resource groups to stimulate discussions about what it means to be confident at work, and have a disability or health condition. In order to help start such a conversation we asked a number of individuals their views:

"It would be liberating to start a fresh conversation. It allows us to hand back responsibility for the workplace adjustment process to the business leaving us to discuss what choices we make that help and hinder our life and work goals – and then what we do about it."

"I like the concept of a 'disability confident employee' because it creates a common language and it is a term to explain what a disabled employee can or should reasonably expect to receive from others. It creates a level of expectation for the employer to live up to."

"It would be hard to get right – and it would have to come with a strong message that we have a long way to go to get a level playing field – I still cannot access the company website – but maybe we convey we have low expectations too when we get stuck with excuses about broken systems without the authority or resources to do anything about it."

Building on the conversations, here are our suggestions about the characteristics that make up a confident disabled employee:

Managing impairment and securing adjustments (if needed)

This means:
- Knowing how to manage impairment while maximizing contribution at work
- Understanding that asking for an adjustment is just an enabling part of the process in wanting to deliver one's best at work
- Being able to make choices and requests for help, such as adjustments, if/when needed

Being yourself

This means:
- Feeling able to share information about disability/health condition with the employer in the expectation that they will want to make the adjustments and being prepared to talk and negotiate about what that might mean to find the win/win
- Feeling confident that people will recognise that disability and impairment might be an important part of who you are, but it doesn't have to define you

- Feeling confident that you can be authentic, be who you really am, and not have to act to hide your impairment

Being expectant and positive (even if you occasionally experience the opposite)

This means:
- Feeling confident that your employer and colleagues will focus on what you can do and not what you cannot do
- Being able to 'work around' any human resisters in way that feels 'good enough' and without derailing your personal journey of building resilience
- Helping people to know your limitations, and trusting that they will work around them just as well as you do

Understanding that the process of building resilience and confidence can take time

This means:
- Understanding that the experience of impairment is common and natural though can sometimes take time to make sense of
- Learning the skills to build resilience to and to side-step occasional pity and low expectation

---

"This kind of 'model' of understanding individual disability confidence would provoke real conversations about how individuals can build resilience at work."

"It would be foolhardy for us to take the pressure off improving recruitment policies – but that doesn't stop us stimulating a brand new debate about the individual actions we have to take to flourish and succeed at work."

"This is helpful – it supports the need to have a common understanding about where we might unintentionally hold ourselves back and what we can do about it."

"This moves us away from being people "needing help" to being the drivers of our career, our destiny, our contribution at work."

Appendix six

The role of charities and advice giving agencies

"What people in the world think of you is really none of your business."
—Martha Graham

Our research showed that one in five of the survey respondents had sought advice from external agencies before deciding whether to share information with their employer. This means that external advice providers are an important source of influence for some people in making a decision to share information.

Advice can confirm or challenge an individual's 'world-view'. Balance, tone and risk are all factors which must be considered.

To further explore this we conducted a 'mystery shopping' exercise with 30 of the UK's charities and advice-giving agencies. We wanted to get a feel for the type of advice that is given on the subject of sharing information about disability and ill-health as well as how far the advice given encouraged people to seek out and secure the workplace adjustments they might need and how they did so.

We looked at their external websites and written information leaflets and tested the balance of information provided to their clients / enquirers about the subject.

The role, purpose and scope of the organisations we looked at were all different. Their 'audiences' also varied between the organisations. Similarly the provision of advice, or not, varied between the organisation depending on the key stakeholder and size of the organisation.

While this was a limited exercise we thought it would be a helpful one to test out the overall 'tone' of advice available to people in work who may look outside of that provided by their employer when deciding whether to share information. We particularly wanted to see whether it matched the desire and ambition of many of the project employer partners who want to secure accurate data in order to better plan for employee need and improve engagement.

Creating the right 'tone' of advice, as well providing accurate content are important elements in helping people to be protected from discrimination and gain access to information that might support them to secure the adjustments they might need.

The right tone and content can also provide opportunities to convey powerful messages that building individual confidence and resilience to 'rehearse' and 'practice' conversations at work is as natural and normal as it gets.

We came across a number of good examples where advice-giving agencies clearly understand employer drivers and the appetite that many have to make the right adjustments people need.

However we equally came across a number of examples that signaled a degree of 'nervousness'. And while advice giving agencies have to weigh up the potential risks that come from giving inaccurate advice where it may lead to someone feeling vulnerable and at risk when sharing information, equally there is a risk in providing advice that suggests disability or ill-health is a secret or big piece of news.

We came across a smattering of examples that conveyed a 'world-view' that suggested employers would, more often than not, react with caution or with punitive measures.

The reality is that advice-giving agencies will hear the difficult examples such as the one we described earlier in Gilly's story – and they are on the front-end hearing from people who might feel insecure particularly in periods of low employment and/or austerity. However, finding the right balance is critical – getting it wrong could be a huge disservice to many UK employers who want to tap into the talent pool of disabled people and retain their people through periods of ill-health and disability.

Here are some of the messages we found on websites and in written information:

> "There are no 'rules' regarding the disclosure of disability."
>
> "Disclosure is a 'tricky business' because it might stigmatise someone with a disability and leads people to stay in the closet."
>
> "Disclosure is not mandatory, however if an individual does disclose the employer has a legal duty to provide reasonable adjustment."
>
> "Individuals do not have to disclose their (health condition) during the recruitment process, but by doing so they will not be protected by the Equality Act."
>
> "Individuals with (health condition) are advised not to share this information at interview. Ensure you have the job first."
>
> "Keep at it, and don't disclose that you have (health condition) until you really feel that you need to."
>
> "Although individuals are under no obligation to tell their employer, it may be helpful or necessary to do so (particularly to receive any reasonable adjustments)."
>
> "I found sharing my diagnosis of (health condition) with my work colleagues a great relief."

Some ideas to try

We invited Paul Farmer, Chief Executive, Mind and Liz Sayce, Chief Executive, Disability Rights UK to help us craft some ideas for advice giving agencies and not-for-profit organisations. This is what we offer:

Think carefully about the tone you want to create – and then set it
- Consider the downside in using the language of 'disclosure' and 'declaration' – it can create the impression that people have a secret or a big piece of news
- Ensure that the advice offered is balanced and includes reference to the importance and value in being yourself at work
- Consider the use of appropriate humour and offer opportunities to help people become less daunted

Create some practical advice and tools for people wanting to learn how to share information
- Consider developing a 'tool-box' of ideas about how to share information (as much or more often than whether to)
- Use real-life stories of people who have gone through the process and out the other side which have a particularly powerful effect or positive outcome
- Offer examples of the types of workplace adjustments that are available from actual named employers. It is a good way of helping individuals see this is a normal part of business life

Encourage and equip front-line advice staff to …
- Encourage advice seekers to think through what they hope for from being open, what the risks might be, whether there are ways to manage those risks (for instance, in how you talk to a line manager about a mental health impairment)
- Help advice seekers to think through the pros and cons but don't over dwell on the cons
- Support enquirers to reflect on the fact that sharing information is unlikely to be a one-off event – it is more likely to be an ongoing feature of someone's life – practicing how to shape your story is an essential component in building resilience and confidence
- Experience the growth and expansion of employees networks and resource groups and growing conversations between disabled employees via these mechanisms, as well as through social media, peer support networks and disabled people's organisations.

> "Organisations led by people with lived experience of disability can encourage and support people in deciding not just 'whether' to be open at work about their lives, but how, when and to whom. Being open can improve our well-being and productivity – and all advice agencies can offer support."—Liz Sayce, Chief Executive, Disability Rights UK

The author

Photo by Bill Knight

Kate Nash OBE is the UK's lead consultant and trainer in the establishment and delivery of workplace disability networks and resource groups. The reach of these networks extends to several thousands of disabled employees; and the successful establishment of networks, and the creation of the right tone, is having a powerful effect on the vision and ambition of disabled talent across the business and public sector.

Nash started her early career supporting disabled people to set up self-help support groups. She has worked in many disability organisations and was Chief Executive of Radar between 2001–2007. She chaired the merger between Radar, Disability Alliance and National Centre for Independent Living in 2012.

After a long successful career campaigning for legislative change she now supports people to be themselves at work, ask for the adjustments they need and helps employers mine their talent and develop their success. Kate Nash Associates has more recently become the 'go-to' provider of personal effectiveness training and development for employees. Their growing suite of workshops and training courses such as Telling Stories for Success and Chain Reaction enable people to get ahead at work.

Nash has helped thousands of disabled people to notice the soft bigotry of low expectation that often comes from many significant others, including work colleagues and one's dearest loved ones. She supports individuals to protect themselves from the low expectation of others. Her experience is that it can often be the first step for disabled employees to get the workplace adjustments they may need and in building a successful and fulfilling career. It can galvanise individuals and enable them to offer exceptional contributions to UK employers looking for diverse talent.

Having campaigned for many years for equalities legislation for disabled people she was awarded an OBE in 2007 for services to disabled people.

www.ingramcontent.com/pod-product-compliance
Lightning Source LLC
Chambersburg PA
CBHW041127300426
44113CB00003B/90